tell me where it hurts

POETRY, MEDITATIONS, & DIVINELY-INSPIRED LOVE NOTES

tasha hunter

AUTHOR OF *What Children Remember: A Memoir*

FIRST EDITION Printed in the United States of America www.tashahunterlcsw.com

Paperback: ISBN 978-1-7344178-4-5
Hardcover ISBN: 978-1- 7344178-5-2
eBook ISBN: 978-1-7344178-6-9

tasha hunter books may be purchased for educational, business, or sales promotional use. For information, please email the author at tashahunterauthor@gmail.com.

Library of Congress Control Number: 2024913555

Cover Design: Simon Walker
Interior Layout: Jana Rade

Admiration

tell me where it hurts by Tasha Hunter is a compelling invitation. It is the kind of invitation that draws you in with warmth and the sacred exhale of feeling our shared humanity. Tasha generously invites us into her pain, and therefore into becoming sacred witnesses of our own. Tasha gives the reader the sweet relief of not being alone in our pain. We find instead an honest and loving guide, who is not afraid to tell us where she hurts. Tasha gently beckons the reader forward, and to keep healing. As you progress through her beautiful and vulnerable words, it is like witnessing the slow warmth of a sunrise. It starts small, seemingly far away, until you realize that everything is now covered in warmth and light. *tell me where it hurts* is an experiential and poetic walk into healing that leaves you wanting to pass along the same gift to others. It is rare that a book itself can make you feel less alone in the world, but Tasha Hunter has accomplished just that.

Monica Dicristina, MA, LPC
Therapist, Author, Podcast Host

In *tell me where it hurts,* Tasha bravely cuts herself open and lays bare for the reader to see and feel the deepest most intimate parts of her pain, pleasure and ultimate healing. Her story becomes our own as Tasha's raw vulnerability gives us permission to fully feel and name every aspect of our own hurt in this shared human experience, knowing we are not alone in the hardest parts of our story. Her words create a safe space as she gently guides readers to feel their own suffering while she offers a healing salve of enduring love, listening and acceptance. Make no mistake, this offering is not a linear remedy or magic potion to numb the pain, but a circular voyage of healing again and again. This book is a companion you will want to keep returning home to when you need to feel seen, held, and heard by someone who offers every bit of herself to her readers.

Andrea Miller, Podcast Host HerStory Speaks, Somatic Coach, Author of *LiBerating Eve* to be released fall 2024

What I can always trust about anything Tasha creates is that the person she truly is will translate to the page. *tell me where it* hurts is Tasha incarnate – vibrant, deeply vulnerable and

beautifully generous. This book of divinely inspired contemplations is a wonderful and wise companion to all wanderers and sojourners en route to find their true North.

Marcie Alvis Walker, author of *Everybody Come Alive: A Memoir in Essa*

For those who want company along their healing journeys, *tell me where it hurts* is a must read! Tasha Hunter offers us the fruits of her fierce and tender labor: seeds of love amidst her traumatic wounding, how she tapped into her innate wisdom as she tended those seeds, and how those seeds continue to blossom into the deliciousness of self-love, partner-love, and community-love. I look forward to sharing with clients and loved ones alike!

Jessica Finney, LMFT, IFS trainer, and fellow truth teller

Tasha Hunter's poignant book is a guiding light for trauma survivors seeking their path back to love. With profound insight and compassion, Hunter weaves together wisdom and personal experience, offering solace and hope to those navigating the journey of healing and recovery. Her words resonate deeply, reminding us that even in our shadow, love is a beacon of healing and restoration. A must-read for anyone on the path to reclaiming their inner strength and embracing the transformative power of love.

Candace Oglesby, Founder, Jurnee Mental Health Consulting

Tasha Hunter's book is a beautiful illustration of the transcendent power of the written word. Using the intricacies of her own experience, her words engage a raw honesty and openness that allows readers to feel seen, embraced, understood and encouraged. I highly recommend this book for all hearts in search of connection.

Courtney Reid LMSW, Licensed Therapist

Tasha Hunter is love personified. Reading *tell me where it hurts* feels like being wrapped in a long, soft, warm hug from someone who knows you've been through it and feels your pain. As you read her beautiful words, you can't help but melt in her arms and let your emotions flow. When you get to the last page—and she lets go, gently holds you by the shoulders, and looks kindly into your eyes—you'll believe healing and liberation are possible.

Marla Taviano, author of *unbelieve, jaded, and whole*

Tasha's writings, reflections and personhood
truly illustrate the paradox of becoming.

Rachael Ringwood, LCSW

In *tell me where it hurts,* Hunter breaks new ground with this poetic approach to healing. Her understanding of suffering caused by unresolved trauma and her powerful insight into our natural desire for growth compelled me to make real and lasting changes in how I think about emotionally charged memories. Tasha is a wise and trustworthy guide to freedom from the bonds that can keep us from experiencing peace. The healing to come from this book will undoubtedly impact many generations. My family has already benefited in immeasurable ways by my own reading of Tasha's work of heart.

Rachel Macy Stafford, New York Times Bestselling author, speaker, & certified special education teacher

My goodness, what can I say, Tasha has gifted us with a masterpiece of love! Love in every sense of the word. Tasha's energy, heartbreak, grief, loss, rising, healing, and finding love took me on such a spiritual and emotional journey. This book brings you directly to your heart. You will be broken open by its words in such profound and medicinal ways. I felt so much resonance in Tasha's journey in all her writings in excavating the wound, navigating childhood trauma and persevering in ways I still wonder about. How did we ever make it here? Too many favorite pieces to name throughout this book. I love how Tasha envisioned this book giving us hope throughout, especially the end. She ended in love. I was in tears in the end when she mentioned that she will teach us everything she knows, vows to give away what she has, because she plans on taking nothing to her Soul's next destination. Our time here is ephemeral, and this isn't our final destination, as Tasha mentioned. I'm so excited for this love offering to be in the world. This was a blessing, just like Tasha. Congratulations, dear friend. I love you. Thank you for telling the world how to love you, too.

Natalie Y. Gutierrez, Author of *The Pain We Carry:*
Healing from Complex PTSD for People of Color

Dedication

To every person who has loved me and to those I have loved, may all
we shared be blessed and forgiven.

To four-year-old Tasha, eight-year-old Tasha, and twelve-year old
Tasha, you will not always face life alone. Love and Safety will come,
and they will stay.

To all the previous versions of me, I love you.

To my suicidal parts, there will come a time when you will be
transformed to life—that time is now. Thank you for seeing my pain
and trying to protect me from it all—I got it now.

To all my traumatized friends, this is for us.

Dear Beautiful One,

I am full of profound gratitude and purpose as I write this letter. My thoughts are with *you all*, (the readers), who will undoubtedly bring my book to life. I began writing **tell me where it hurts** more than four years ago. This collection of thoughts, meditations, quotations, and poems became a safe space for all the thoughts and feelings that had nowhere else to go.

I wrote this for you, for me, and for *us*.

I hope you'll pick up this book when you need deep resonance and an even deeper truth for your experiences. Perhaps you'll quote it to your friends, clients, and across social media and we'll hear it discussed on podcasts, IG Lives, book clubs, and in creative writing classes. In my dreams, **tell me where it hurts** will be your go-to gift for siblings, girlfriends, and best friends.

I have poured my heart and soul into the following pages. Every pain, tension, and lesson learned—it's all here. I've infused each chapter with vulnerability and authenticity to allow you to see yourself in my writing. While reading, I hope you find moments that resonate deeply—where you feel seen, understood, and less alone. I hope it becomes the companion that reminds you that you deserve love and respect. That my truth becomes a shared and collective truth for all of us.

The following pages are for the traumatized, heartbroken, overwhelmed, tired, sad, lonely, numb, and anyone who's doing their best. This book is also for the survivors among us, the thrivers, rebellious ones, agitators, disrupters, generational curse-breakers, activists, truth-tellers, the ones who can't be bought or bribed, troublemakers, those who will *not* remain silent, those who are intuitive, seekers, helpers, introverts, neurodivergent, queer, trans, nonbinary, two-spirited, highly sensitive, outcasts, adoptees, and orphans.

You all are my people.

May my words become the bridge that leads us to each other.

I've organized this book into three sections. First, *Excavating the Wound* is where the depth of my pain lays bare before you. Next, *Tending to the Wound* encapsulates the lessons I'm

learning as I continue to liberate myself from the trauma. Finally, *Healing the Wound* is the sweetest spot—where I am free and unapologetic.

Thank you for embarking on this journey with me. I pray that my words will find their way into your hearts and stay with you long after you finish reading the final page.

With love and gratitude,

tasha hunter

Manifestation

This is my
hope,
prayer,
love letter,
offering, and
testimony.

This is a gift to all my traumatized friends.
This is my legacy
and my communal offering.
This is how I memorialize my trauma
and my liberation.

I *see* you.
I *know* you.
I *am* you.

May the words that have
poured from my heart
act as a vessel and pour into yours.
May you receive them.

May they be a strong shoulder to cry on,
the ear that never tires of listening,
the kiss before you drift off to sleep, and
the hand you hold in your darkest hour.

May my words
be a balm,
a salve,
and even a potion
for your tender heart.

I love you.

I.
Excavating
the Wound

The Bones of Trauma

You were starving, emaciated.
Bones nearly breaking through thin skin.
But I didn't feed you.

You were bleeding,
hemorrhaging. Your
body seizing.
Still, I didn't stitch you.

You were out of oxygen, panting,
wheezing, and coughing up blood.
I never tried to save you.

You needed attention.
But I ignored you.

You needed community.
I kept you isolated.

You needed encouragement.
I attacked.
You needed accountability
and justice.
But I blamed you
for what *I* did
to you.

Holidays

I

It's seven p.m., and I've just taken
my first sip of water.
My body is starving, but not for food...
I've spoken but haven't been understood.
I've been visible yet remain unseen.

It's the holidays for everyone except me,
and it's no wonder
tears fall as I prepare a dinner
that will likely end up in the trash.
My appetite is ravenous
for food made by the hands of a loved one.
My body is longing to be touched.

Somebody call 9-1-1.

I've forgotten to drink.
I've forgotten to eat.
I'm wasting away.
All while willing myself
to remember
how to breathe.

Can anyone remind me how it feels to be loved?

Say Her Name

I sat with my grief
until
she held up a sign
that said:
belonging.

I sat with my grief
until
she whimpered,
mother.

I sat with my grief
until
she sobbed,
father.

I sat with my grief
until
she screamed,
family!

I sat with my grief
until
she found what was missing:
love.

Affirmation:
Pause.
Take a deep breath.
Exhale slowly.
Say to yourself, "I am worthy of the love that I desire."

Conversations with Grief

 I told my grief:
She's too much,
too heavy,
too all-consuming
all the damn time.

It's like I've trudged through the Arizona desert
with a 100-pound duffel.
I can't be expected to keep on
carrying her. Doesn't she know when
enough is enough?

The pain is too much.
The enormity of it all
makes me want to drop it *all* off
on a remote island
never to be felt, thought of, or experienced again.

I need to feel something else besides sadness; besides this
hopelessness that won't let me loose.

I wish I could escort my pain to the front row
of my life so that she can see what else I'm made of besides grief—

so she can see that love and joy also have places in my life.

Being Human

Life is all about
going through shit.
Making the best of shit.
Being okay with shit.
Numbing from shit.
Being happy about shit. Being tired of the bullshit.
Being in some shit.
Getting out of shit.
Fighting over stupid shit.
Laughing over shit.
Talking shit. Hiding shit.
Daydreaming about shit.
Holding onto shit.
Taking a shit.
Listening to some shit.
Healing from shit. Coping with shit.
Apologizing for shit.
Loving shit. Hating shit.
Denying shit.
Ruining shit. Creating shit.
Scheduling shit.
Giving a shit. Being about that shit.
Crying over shit.
Thinking about shit.
Sleeping on shit.
Doing shit. Avoiding shit.
Trying shit. Being a shit.
Running from shit.
Manifesting shit. Praying for shit.
Ain't life some shit?
Fuck this shit.

No Inspector Gadget

Some things will be different.
Some of it won't make sense.
How did we get *here*?
I try to release myself from the obligation to solve mysteries.
I wasn't created to be a detective of other people's truths.

**My mind keeps making up stories to replace
the truth hidden inside you.
I don't know why we haven't talked.
What I do know is... I miss you.**

The Ending

Each morning, I wake
with one question:
"How could I have
prevented *this*?"
There will be no answers,
no resolution.

Prayer

"Better exists for everyone
else. I want better, *too*.
Show me the way."

Post-traumatic Truth

What didn't kill me
almost killed me, and
could still kill me.

What didn't kill me
inflicted me with depression, anxiety, and PTSD.

What didn't kill me
led me to unhealthy relationships,
body dysmorphia, body hatred, self-harm,
disordered eating, and neglectful self-care.

What didn't kill me *didn't* make me stronger.
Instead, it made me pretend to be strong.
It made me into a professional masker.

No one needs trauma to make them stronger—
to build character or tenacity, either.

Love is enough.
Love strengthens.
Love builds.
Love is life.

Let's tell the truth about trauma.

"Family"

Something bad happened, and I built
up the courage to talk about it.
I reached out for help.

But you didn't pick up the phone.
You didn't reply to my text.
You didn't comment or react to my post.

You stayed silent during my unraveling.

You knew about it, but you didn't say anything.
Instead?
You prepared a table and broke
bread with my abuser.

That's how I knew you were fake as fuck,
and that I'd never speak to you again.
You could have stopped it from happening...
But you were on your bullshit.

Where do I go when love feels like it is in short supply?

I want to exist in your truth, in the deepest well of your authenticity. But if I can't—we will not exist at all.

1,000 Times a Day

I ask myself:

Why did they leave?
Why did they ghost?
Why didn't they communicate?
Why did they see me as
expendable—something to be
discarded?
Why didn't they listen?
Why didn't they defend me?

Why did *they* change?
Why did they stay the same?
Why did they hurt me?
Why did they lie?
Why did they abuse me?
Why did they stay silent?

999 times, I know I'll never
receive the answers,
and as I use my hand to gently
draw circles around my heart,
I rest in the knowledge that one day

I will heal from this, too.

Resilient

Surviving is the minimum.
It is *not* enough.
Someone should pay me reparations,
especially after
all I've been through.

When they decided to leave,
did they realize it would
take the rest of my life
to learn how to exist
without them?

No Compromise

I want to matter,
but I don't want to lose myself
in the comfort of their acceptance.

I want to belong
without the expectation
to conform
or
violate my own authenticity.

Hindsight Is...

All I know
is that I love you—
always have,
always will.
I regret that we
didn't know how to grow,
to heal.
We didn't know how to speak
or how to listen
to each other.

We gave it our all.
We didn't know that there was *more*.
We didn't know what
we didn't know...
We were terrified of vulnerability,
longing for more
and hurting while pushing away the pain.

I wish I had known how to become
the medicine we both needed.
You tried to tell me.
I tried to tell you.
And still, we missed each other...
I wish I knew how to be different,
how to change,
how to love me and you better,
and because I can't go back in time
I'll die with a thousand regrets for a thousand years
because I still love you.
I will *always* love you.

The Cycle

I try to tell you how I feel.
"I hope I don't sound childish."

I try to tell you the truth.
"I hope I don't hurt your feelings."

I try to answer your questions.
"I hope you don't leave me."

I try to respond to every insecurity.
"I hope you will trust me."

I try to introduce you to my people.
"I hope you will see the importance of being in community."

I have tried too many things
to be in a relationship with you—
too much contorting,
too much stretching,
too much labor and codependency
masked as love and devotion.

I hope you forgive me for doing what is best for both of us.

Prayer.

May the universe that is healing me
heal you too.
May the universe that cares for me
care for you too.
May we forgive each other for what we didn't know
how to fix at the time.
May we cherish the good and never forget the lessons.
May we both find the love that we deserve.

Misfortune Told

When you say, "I don't want to hurt you."
I hear, "I know I'm going to hurt you—brace for impact."

What if you said, "I'm going to love you. I'm
going to be honest with you"
instead of preparing me for all the ways you're going to devastate me.

I don't want a love that makes me feel like I'm *not* loved.

It is not enough to say I love you when you won't stop the hurting long enough to start the healing that can reveal to you what loving even means.

Hello

Love is not supposed to feel:

- Shaky
- Uncertain
- Avoidant
- Out of control
- Self-conscious
- Unpredictable
- Controlling
- Sad
- Panicked
- Paranoid
- Dismissive
- Manipulative

None of that's love.
Instead, it's your childhood trauma calling.

Pick up the phone.

Life Reminders

1. If they are not pouring love into you,
    they are taking it away—
    Depart from the energy vampires.

2. Let your goodbyes heal you and expose the woundedness
    and need for healing that exists within them.

3. People are thinking of you a lot less and a lot more
    than you realize. You cannot control
    a single bit of it—so you may as well show up and stop
    shrinking.

4. You have been shut down and shut out—
    this is not the end of your story.

You know what's heartbreaking?
The amount of time I spend thinking
about how to prevent myself from dying
of a broken heart.

Anti-Blackness

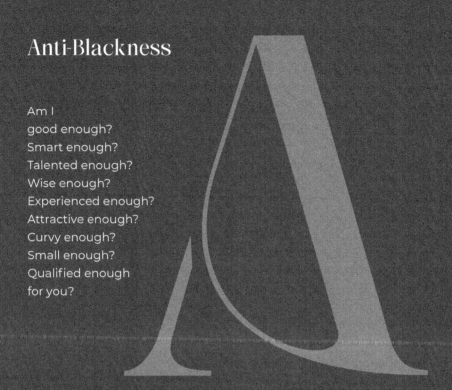

Am I
good enough?
Smart enough?
Talented enough?
Wise enough?
Experienced enough?
Attractive enough?
Curvy enough?
Small enough?
Qualified enough
for you?

Dear White Supremacy Culture:

I will not hate myself
or change myself to be accepted by you.
I will not deny any parts of myself.
I will not ignore my history.
I will not silence my voice.
I will not give up on my dreams.
I will not be controlled or intimidated by you.
I will not adopt or mimic your ways.
I will not turn away from my community.
I will not prioritize whiteness.

Unnecessary Shame

It is not shameful to need
connection, intimacy, belonging,
support and authentic concern,
freedom, ease, rest.

It is not shameful to need people
who share the unspoken experiences or to yearn
for a safe container, away from the
expectations of others,
a place where you don't have to be "on," existing
in other people's version of good or perfect.

You and your needs are not shameful.
The fact that your needs
have not been met—that is the shame.

What are your needs?
Examples: emotional safety, intimacy, close-knit
community, loving partnership, child-like fun, rest,
respected boundaries, understanding, love, etc.

List a few here:

- _____

- _____

- _____

- _____

Major Anxiety

Are we okay? Did I do something wrong?
Did I say something wrong?
Are you ghosting me? Are you going to give up on me?
Are you going to turn on me?
Are you lying to me?

Do you *really* care about me?
Do you want to spend time with me? Do you love me?

I hope you know how much you mean to me.
Will I be okay? Will I survive?
I hope I don't die. I won't survive this.
Am I sick? Do I have cancer? When will I die?

Am I safe? Is someone going to rob me, rape me, or kill me?
Is someone going to steal my ideas, my words, my work?
Is someone going to take advantage of me?
Are they going to hurt me?
Can I take care of myself?
Will my bills be paid?

Why am I doing this?
What if I fail? What if no one supports me?
What if I look like a fool? What if I'm making the wrong decision?
I hope I remember to do _____.
What if I'm missing out on what's for me?
What if I don't have the right information?
Who can I call to help me? Is anybody there for me?
Will anyone like it? Share it? Review it?
Will anyone see my value?
Do I matter?

So Afraid

Anytime I'm in a predominately white space, I ask myself, "Am I safe?"
Anytime I'm in a predominantly Black space, I ask myself, "Am I safe?"

Anytime I'm in a room with cis-hetero men, I ask myself, "Am I safe?"
Anytime I'm in a room with cis-hetero
women, I ask myself, "Am I safe?"

Anytime I'm in a public space, I ask myself, "Am I safe?"
Anytime I'm in a religious space, I ask myself, "Am I safe?"

Anytime I drive, I ask myself, "Am I safe?"
Anytime I'm alone at home, I ask myself, "Am I safe?"
Am I safe from racism?
Am I safe from terrorists?
Am I safe from homophobia?
Am I safe from fatphobia?
Am I safe from colorism?
Am I safe from sexual assault?
Am I safe from robbery?

Is *anyone* safe?

Hiding

All of the good work I've done,
all of the relationships I've built,
all of the energy I've put into helping others
won't matter one bit if I continue to stay silent
about *my* suffering.

Some people have hurt me, and it feels as if I may never recover.
Knowing that these wounds have no expiration date
hurts more than what they did to me.

Dear Reader,

Use the space below to write a short letter of hope, freedom, and encouragement to yourself.

Dear _____

_____

_____

_____

_____

_____

_____

_____

_____

_____

_____

Don't Leave

Please don't leave me.
When this relationship ends,
I can't tell whether it is

my fault,

my karma,

or my destiny...

No matter how we ended, I will love you into eternity.

Anxious-Avoidant Type

A part of me will always remain close to an exit plan,
ready to leave at a moment's notice.
Lifejacket on underneath
all the layers,
oxygen mask and compass
in my back pocket.

Just in case I find myself on a sinking ship.

I don't need a reason,
just a feeling.
It's not personal,
just strategically designed by a lifetime of trauma.

Rescue

It's hard to sleep when I'm singing
everyone else a sweet lullaby.

Everyone else is provided
safety equipment, while mine is broken.

**How do I plan to save my own life? First,
notice how I care for myself:**

1. Waking after a night of slumber, thanks to PP&P
   (People of TikTok, perimenopause, and PTSD), I take
   a sip of water from the glass on my bedside table.
2. Tell the Creator "thank you" for presence, purpose, provision,
   and protection. It's a miracle that my heart keeps beating.
3. Preheat the cast iron skillet. Remind the part of me
   that replaces nourishment with checking emails
   that I need bacon—Smithfield's Thick Cut—along
   with a bowl of buttery grits and a flaky biscuit split
   in half, topped with butter and grape jelly.
4. Help myself before I help others. Cambio
   Dark Roast with caramel creamer.
5. Motivate and encourage myself: "Alexa,
   play *Usher Radio* on Pandora."
6. Shower. Will it be Bronner's Peppermint Castille,
   Dove Deep Moisture, or Dr. Teal's Glow and Radiance?
   A clean body makes room for a clean mind.
7. Notice when my skin is dryer instead of softer. Notice
   when my body is dehydrated, skin cracked, peeling, and
   dull. Why do I neglect the only body I'll ever have? This
   is a sign that I'm not loving myself enough. I grab the
   whipped shea butter, cocoa butter, coconut oils, and
   Jergens lotion—wherever my hand lands first. I ask my
   body for forgiveness. I love my skin—I should be kinder to
   it. What else does she need? I drink water—dehydration
   leads to ashy, peeling skin. I notice I'm hungry, thirsty,
   and longing for warmth, softness, and attention. I make
   a ritual of giving this to myself and my skin... *first*.

8. Pull an affirmation card—what does Oprah
    or Louise Hay have to say to me today?
9. Sit silently. What do my ancestors and spirit guides
    need me to remember? Clarity comes.
10. Open my laptop and write. Ask for space from the parts
    of me who are convinced I have nothing good to say.
11. Check on my friends and family—they remind me
    that I'm loved and that my life gives them life.

How I plan to save my life:

- _____

- _____

- _____

- _____

- _____

- _____

- _____

- _____

- _____

- _____

- _____

I've spent too much of my life either chasing love or running away from it.

Soft whisper:

May I be captured.
May I be captured.
May I be captured...
by love.

They Didn't Care

It took me a minute to realize
it wasn't that my voice didn't matter.
My voice was never the problem.

It was the fact that for a long time,
I was surrounded by people who
plugged their ears just so they could say, "I didn't hear you."

They covered their eyes so they could say, "I didn't see anything."

They kept their distance so they could say, "I didn't know."

They feigned ignorance so they could say, "I
didn't understand, and still don't."

They were fake as fuck in moments when I
was the most naked and vulnerable.

Questions with No Answers

Will *Final Destination* be the cause of my death?
(Cue the scene with the log truck on the interstate).

Will endangered animals be saved?

Are my prayers powerful enough to stop rape,
child abuse, drug trafficking, or war?

Will politicians ever choose *us* over them?

Will Beyonce, Meg, and Oprah be more
respected in death than in life?

Will my writing reach one million people?

Whose God is real?
Am I real?

Will he continue loving me?
Will she continue loving me?

Is the imaginary hell worse than Earth's hell?

Will I fall and break my hip when I'm older?
Who will take care of me when I can no longer take care of myself?

Will scientists ever agree to release the cure for cancer?
What natural, normal human condition will be pathologized next?

Will God come back to Earth like a thief in the night?

Will white supremacy ever end?

Message to Little Tash

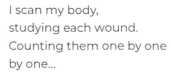

I scan my body,
studying each wound.
Counting them one by one
by one...

My body is a vessel for stories
that I'll never speak.

What can I take away from this
violence?

That the people who've cut me the deepest
aren't reliable sources of information
about who I am?

That I can't believe the words
of people
who have loved me
the least?

That I can't depend on the ones
who were silent when I needed them the most?

Shepherdess

As sad as it is to admit,
I wasn't born into the wrong family.

My birth wasn't a mistake.

I'm not a black
sheep, either.

I came into the world
to stop the hurting,
to expose the secrets,
to deliver the healing.

To tell the truth.

Someone needed to speak
so I became the courage they lacked.

The one with the voice.
The feeder of truth.
The protector of the vulnerable ones
under my care.

Emotionally Abusive Mothers

We who were raised by monsters
fear that we may turn into monsters too.
This fear corrupts and interrupts
how we give and receive love,
distances us from loving ourselves
This fear, though, is in part what keeps us
human...
We represent all they wished they could be.

**I still need someone to be my mother.
I still need someone to be my father.**

Parenting myself isn't enough.

**On the hard days, it is hard to decide
whether my life matters at all.**

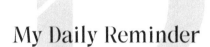

My Daily Reminder

Because there are no guarantees,
much less a roadmap.

Because life is hard,
but being human is harder.

Because situations are ever-changing, while happiness is fleeting.

Because so much is out of my control,
the answers aren't always clear.

I'm doing the best that I can.
I'll make mistakes,
even piss people off.

I will fail and disappoint.

I'm going to hurt others, too.

On most days, though, I'm doing the best that I can.

Lion's Rebellion

If I don't speak,
they'll rewrite my
her-story.

They'll say it didn't happen,

leave out the crimes
they committed.

They'll say I'm being *too dramatic*,
or that they *don't remember*.

They hope I don't remember either,
praying that I keep their truth
hidden in the dark corners.

Takers

As if
I haven't lost
enough,
you keep finding new ways
to take more.

Is my skin not enough?
Would you like my bones spread on a silver platter, too?
Strewn across a bed of arugula, served cold
with a light, lemony vinaigrette.

You ask me to
stay warm,
stay sweet,
stay giving.
All while you
suck the marrow out of my life.

Were you expecting me to not notice your emotional cannibalism?

Relationship Boundaries

No more once-a-year text messages.
No more text-only conversations and relationships.
No more group-chat-only friendships.

In this stage of my existence, I require
depth,
vulnerability,
people with capacity and willingness for more,
family,
real, intentional community,
partnerships and allies.

People who see *me* as much as I see *them*.

Acquaintances aren't enough and have never been enough.
No more social media lurkers—I need encouragement
and validation of my sharing.
I have a zero-tolerance policy against surface-level interactions.
I deserve more because I give the most.

What Do You Deserve from Others?

- _____

- _____

- _____

- _____

- _____

Social Media

Sometimes, I wish I could tell all the pretty-book-cover authors,
all the TikTok-famous mental health advocates and
all the armchair trauma experts

to tell the fucking truth about trauma.
That sometimes
it doesn't get better.

Sometimes, there is *NO* better.
That sometimes
the hurt will keep hurting.

This is what it means to tell
the unfortunate truth.
Even when it's scary,
when it's inconvenient,

Tell it.

Being Love

I didn't come from love.
I had to create it
like Clair Huxtable in the Cosby family
preparing dinner after a long day at the office,
with arms
that give hugs and kisses to my little family.
A firm voice of protection to anyone trying to hurt me and mine.
Making home special for neighborhood kids, in-laws, and passersby.
Never too busy to open my heart and allow my love to propagate.

Like Evelyn Couch in *Fried Green Tomatoes*,
visiting her friend, Ninny, at the nursing home.
Day after day, listening to my friends give an account
of joy, pain, sorrow, laugh-out-loud gossip sessions, and amens.

"That motherfucker!"

Plan trips to lie on couches while eating
all the charcuterie, drinking wine and spirits
we can handle, smoking a little *cannaBLISS*,
sending text messages that read:

I love you.

I miss you.

We give each other metaphorical
roses, sunflowers, and daisies while we live
because it's too late in death.
When my friend weeps, I weep. When I weep, she weeps.

Remembering them in the ways that they want to be remembered.
Fighting the patriarchy and standing up
to old, white, racist, bigoted people—
speaking up at Thanksgiving dinner.

Instead of *God Bless America*, we honor and praise
the divine feminine Goddess within us.
We share our secrets and family secrets, too.
The ones that used to cause shame
now empower.

We use our time to build communities, educate, and uplift—paving
the way for others to get free or die trying.

These are the moments we all live for. These are the people
who make life worth living.
Because of them, I am a better mother, partner, friend, and mentor.

Like Mother Maya Angelou giving motherly advice
to Oprah and the world. That soft, stern voice.
I show up for myself and others to make sure we give ourselves
amazing grace when we make mistakes,
break hearts, learn hard lessons.

When I want to sulk and stay in a shame spiral,
I imagine Maya sitting with me in pajamas,
drinking tea and telling me, "Stop it now; stop
your crying—it's going to be okay."

I imagine her telling me to be grateful
that Goddess will take care of me. That kind of love
is what I give myself and what I try to give to each person I encounter.

The Work

The hardest person to forgive is myself—
to change,
to compliment,
to accept or
show mercy to
myself.

The hardest person to listen to is me
in this self-relationship,
alone.
To comfort and
bear witness to
myself.

The hardest person to take care of
to honor,
to protect and
to love is
me.

I want to change that.

To my ancestors, angels, and spirit guides:
make me feel again.

Heal the wounds that are keeping me
disconnected from myself.

Gently weave your spirit through the fibers
of my unhealed trauma
so that what remains is there to set me free.

Lost in Transition

At times,

I feel...

Forgotten.

Invisible.

Lost.

It's as if my personal navigation system
malfunctions and the location can't be found.
Error 404: try again.

Contact your network administrator for further assistance.

To the ones who know my name:
Help me find my way
back
home.

A Letter to Men

Contrary
to the history of the world...

You do not have to kill.
You do not have to start wars.
You do not have to destroy.

Be healed.

You do not have to hurt others to meet your needs.
You do not have to hurt others to survive.
You do not have to hurt others to show your rage.
You do not have to hurt others to exact revenge on your abusers.
You do not have to hurt others to prove your
allegiance to god or your country.
You do not have to kill to prove you're mentally ill.

We *know*.

Church Folk

They say,
"Come as you are."
What they mean is,
Come as you are, but be prepared

to be colonized.
Controlled.
Indoctrinated.

I've never met more people
who are afraid
to be themselves—
to find themselves within
the mystery of the great becoming,

to have their own opinion
or to be different,
to reveal failures and shortcomings
or tell their truth,

to wrestle with
and be honest about questions and doubts—
than in the place that tells us
to come as you are:
Church.

Questions for Goddess

I sometimes wonder
if you want to sue the whole damn world
for defamation, fraud, or
the misrepresentation of your character,
and crimes against humanity all in the name of...

I wonder if you ever want to charge and convict
the unwell ancestors who wrote the stories,
created the books. Those who dictated the laws
and changed the world permanently.

I wonder if you get angry about
all the misrepresentations
of your work, your world, and your word

I wonder if you ever shake your head in disgust
at the violence and apathy,
waiting on us to get *it* right,
get *you* right, and finally
take notice of the little things
and make them bigger things—
so that we can
take notice of the bigger things
and make them non-existent things.

For us to finally figure out
life isn't about what
we were told, taught, or brainwashed to believe.

I wonder if you want to do the whole
Noah-and-the-ark thing again
for good practice.

Raw for You

Would it kill you
to be real?

To trust?
Or cry?

To allow me to sink
into the most vulnerable
parts of you?

I want to be with you
in the thick of it
and in the darkness.

I want to be with you
in the valley
and in the shadows.

After you've allowed
truth to drip
from your lips
I must know...
Did it kill you?

Or
did you
live?

Hiding Yourself from Me

When
awkward air fills the space between us,
when walls replace intimacy and connection,
it's often because
truth is somewhere else
being held hostage.

In the words of Cardi B., "Be careful with me."

When I am alone at the end of my world,
I hope someone remembers
to rescue me.

In Defense of Us

In 1964, Malcolm X said, "The most disrespected person in America is the Black woman. The most unprotected person in America is the Black woman. The most neglected person in America is the Black woman."

I counter that the most *invisible*, *disrespected* person in the world is the Black, queer, single woman who is without a mother, father, sister, or brother.

What they should hate besides queer and trans people:

- **White supremacy culture**
- **Patriarchy**
- **Religion**
- **People who hurt animals**
- **People who destroy trees**
- **People who create meth, crack, and heroin**
- **People who abuse women and children**
- **People who protect abusers**
- **People who rape, murder, and burglarize**
- **People who steal native lands, medicine, and culture**
- **People who profit from oppression**
- **The people who hurt them**
- **The people who taught them to hate**

Lesson #325

Each time I trusted in
someone else's vision for my life,
I lost a piece of my Self.

Each time I prioritized someone else's emotional wellness,
I lost connection to myself.

Each time I relied on someone else to make me whole,
I became
more insecure,

depressed,
anxious,
hopeless.

Each time I adopted someone else's fears,
courage quietly walked out of the door.

Begging You

Please stay with me.
Don't reject or
ghost me.

Please don't block me from being a part of your life.

Please don't give up on me
or turn against me.

Please see me.

Please give me a chance.

Please just *love* me.

**I'm done being in relationships that require me
to follow someone else's moral compass.**

I am my own North Star.

Would you still love
me when...?

I refuse to be the qualities that
you lack within yourself.
I refuse to be the therapist that you need.
I refuse to be the parent, lover, bank, and caretaker.

Will you then start to take care of yourself?
Or am I asking too much?

I gotta save myself.

New Lessons

I've known
fear,
shame,
guilt,
regret,
self-righteousness,
ego-tripping,
rage,
blame,
insecurity,
hopelessness,
grief,
worthlessness,
defensiveness,
learned helplessness,
people-pleasing,
lying,
procrastination,
failure,
and isolation.

Time to learn something different.

Self-Talk

One hundred percent of the time, whenever I said,
"I don't have a choice."
"I'm too old."
"I can't."
"It is what it is."

I had just given up on myself and the hope
that my life could be any different.

I have to remind myself:
I *can* change.
I *can* change.
I *can* change.

What Do I Need to Remind Myself of When Life Is Hard?

- _____

- _____

- _____

- _____

- _____

- _____

- _____

- _____

- _____

- _____

- _____

- _____

- _____

- _____

- _____

**I don't know a single person
who is living
in the absence of purpose and intention
and is happy doing so.**

What is my purpose?

_____

_____

What are my intentions to help me fulfill my purpose?

_____

_____

_____

Reminder:

Pause
Breathe
Hydrate
Stay focused
Stay ready

If Loving Myself Is Wrong...

Why does loving myself feel right *and* wrong at the same time?
Like talking about money, sex, politics, religion, or race
anywhere *but* my home.

Or leaving Target without buying anything.
Showing cleavage in anything with a V-neck.
Sitting on my brand-new couch butt naked.
Telling the Trader Joe's cashier, who looked
sad, "It's going to be okay,"
even though I don't know her like that.

Gathered in my office with five or six other Black people, afraid
that the White supervisor would say
we were being cliquish or showing favoritism.

I found my seat on the airplane in first class,
where I was the only Black person.
Or on that vacation in Denver, smoking the
weed we bought from a dispensary.
Saying "no" to something I definitely do not want to do.
Saying "hello" to a stranger who quickly glanced in my direction
before choosing to avoid eye contact.

I *know* I need love.
I deserve it, *too*.
So why does it feel so damn wrong?

I don't want to be right.

My People

I need
someone who
isn't afraid to speak up for me.

Someone
who ends relationships
with people who mistreat me.

I need
someone
who's willing
to fight anyone
who is abusive towards me.

Someone who will stand beside me
while in the presence of my abuser.

Black, Queer, Orphaned Woman

I can cry, but if I do,
I'm perceived as weak,
or worse,
I'm ignored.

I can tell you the truth,
but if I do, I'm perceived
as being dramatic
or a bitch.

I can scream, but if I do,
I'm perceived as angry
or irrational.

I can go silent, but if I do
I'm perceived as distant
or avoidant.

I can pretend that everything is okay, but if I do
I'm perceived as happy and
"having it all together,"
independent,
self-sufficient,
and not needing anyone.

Parts Work

Are we in danger?
Who do you fear?
Is there a threat?
Is there a crisis?
Is this a trauma response?
Who do you think I am?
What do you need from me?

Goddess,

Please help me to allow the dead things in my life to rest in peace.

**"Some people just get to exist, and they are cared for.
That wasn't ever true for me
because I came into existence.
That was the cause of my invisibility." ~R.R.**

Being born is the cause of my alienation.
Being born is the cause of their departure from all responsibility.
Being born is why they hate me.

May I be reborn into love.

I love you
I love you
I love you

Invisibility

It's not
a matter of
if
I think I'm
worthy.

       That is without question.

I feel the most pain
when I question
if someone
will stick around
long enough
to *see* my worth, too.

Real Talk

I sincerely want
people not to be weird.

By *not weird*, I mean
I want people in my life who can
hold my sadness.
Hold my tenderness.
Hold my grief.

People who can hold a conversation with considerate responses.
And if you don't know what to say,
tell me.
Don't just meet my tears and my stories
with awkward silence,
or even worse,
nervous laughter,
blank stares, or
automatic replies.

My feelings aren't the problem.
It's your fear of feeling
that makes it hard for us
to be in a relationship.

You're busy judging me, while
I'm busy peeling back the layers
of my unhealed trauma.

Don't be fucking weird.

See Me, Hear Me, Understand...

When you speak to me...?

Speak
from your heart.

Speak
so that I can feel you.

Speak
so that I can see
into you.

Speak
so that we can
connect.

Do you know the language of your heart?

We don't need distance and disconnection.

We need love.
I need love.
Talk to me.

Tender Roots

I have not been loved well or cared for
enough,
and I want to be.

I need to be.

This longing is the source and the sum
of all my turmoil.

Loss

Instead of holiday parties,
I wish we could normalize grief parties.

We would get together with our safest people and
wear our favorite pajamas.

We'd go around the room
and share what's breaking our hearts.

We'd pass around the tissues,
while we cry
and rage.

We'd eat our favorite foods
drink and smoke,
and end the night
laughing and singing karaoke.

Dying to Be Free

I'm thankful that I'll die one day.
No more anxiety,
depression,
or oppression.

No more hustling
or labor.

No more loneliness
or trying to fit in.

No more trying to stand out
or trying to garner support.

No more trying to do it alone.

No more struggling
or pressure.

No more erasure.

I'm thankful I'll die one day.

This world is too cold, too hard, too much.

Emotionally Immature Parenting

Stop bleeding on your children
and calling it *love*,
forcing young minds to grow
at an exponentially abnormal rate.

Stop bleeding on your children
and calling it *family*,
forcing them to be
their own safety
because relatives are vultures.

Stop bleeding on your children
and calling it *life*.

One day, your children will grow up and call it
trauma.

Just *stop*.

Un-homed

Arkansas
will always be my birthplace.

The place where parts of me died.
The place where I can easily map
the *whys*, *whens*, *hows*, and *who* did it.

Arkansas will *never* be my home.

Beginner People-Pleasers

Children are labeled as *good*
when they're quiet and don't raise a fuss.
When they don't cry, whine, or throw tantrums.
When they sleep through the night.

When they get older, they're labeled *good*
when they earn high grades, play sports,
and pretend to not be impacted by
the bully, the abuser, or the negligent one.

Children are called *good*
when they're calm and not too emotional in the presence
of all sorts of chaos and dysfunction.

They're rewarded with being the family
favorite, called *mature*, *well-behaved*,
and given more responsibilities.

Children are called *good* when they eat all their food.

Children are called *good* when they put others before themselves,
and when they're sweet and endearing to the family predator.
Parents are often the first advocates for suffering
silently, peacefully, and alone.

I'll never again suffer silently. When I am in pain,
may the world hear my cries.

Question: What do you want to be when you grow up?

A teacher?
A nurse?
An attorney?

Answer: Left alone. I want to be unbothered. I want to be free. I want to know peace and to feel normal. I want to be happy. I want the opportunity to grow up.

To live.

What do you want to be in your next chapter?

- _____

- _____

- _____

- _____

- _____

- _____

F

#8

For most of my life,
I've lived halfway in my body
and halfway gone.

It's taken a lifetime
to convince Little Me
she's safe
and can come out now.

She can be here
fully.

She doesn't have
to go away.

No one is going to hurt her.
Maybe one day, she'll believe me.

Birther

I came into this world
ready to love you.

It's a shame
you never arrived
to receive it.

Kinfolk

There is a common phrase in Black households,
"All *skin*folk ain't *kin*folk."

A part of me wants to be *kinfolk* with everyone.

Everyone doesn't want the same thing, though.

What a shame and loss for all of us.

Surface-level Shit

I asked to go deep, but
she fed me
from the shallowest part
of her.

I asked for the truth, but
she fed me
everything else.

I asked for her heart, but
she fed me
tidbits of artificial additives
Red Dye #3,
Aspartame,
Monosodium Glutamate (MSG),

and she wonders why I'm sick
of her.

What's Love?

Will you love me—

When I need you to love me?

When I say *no*?

When I'm honest?
Busy?
Too quiet?
Tired?

When I'm not laughing or smiling?
Don't want to be touched?
Don't have the right words?

When I'm triggered?

Venting?

When I've changed or
chosen myself?

Rope's End

I'm trying desperately

to hold on,
to not lose you,
to not lose me.

To not lose
what remains after
all the other losses

and the grief,
upon grief,
upon grief.

I'm trying.
I'm trying.
I'm trying
to hold on...

**We always said that we'd still look good, laugh,
and have fun together when *we* turned 75.**

**Now we *are* looking good, laughing, having
fun, and growing older *apart*...
What happened?**

Why Some People Refuse to Heal

Some things have to be broken,
given permission
to fall
completely apart.

Let it.

So that you can see who *and* what is real.

Weaponizing Silence

Silence is a protector or a weapon.

When we ask another person to not speak,
what power do their words hold?

Are we afraid of feeling
too much
sadness?
Grief?
Shame?
Accountability?

Where there is silence, the connection dies.

May we who are hungry for authentic
relating allow our hearts to speak.
May we who are healing allow others to speak and heal, too.

Elder Advice

Belonging...
We all want it. We all need it.

We all deserve it, so we must name it

out loud and often,
to ourselves and then to each other

so none of us feel alone
in our needing.

Calling

I have to remind myself,
whether I'm in the dark
or in the lowest of valleys,
alone in the wilderness
of my experiences

or in the middle of the ocean
fighting to stay afloat

that my life
matters.

Being here is not an unfortunate mistake.

My *well* ancestors keep watch over me,
and because the universe knows my name,
I can ask to be reminded of who I am.

I can ask
to be ushered through the difficult parts of li
for sustenance,
for a loving ally,
and
for wisdom in my life's direction.

I can ask for what I need.

Family Matters

There is a difference
between a relative and family.

Between a person who gave birth
versus a mother or mom.

Between a person who inseminated prostatic fluid
versus a father or dad.

Between having custody of a child
versus being a parent.

One protects.
One prioritizes the social, mental, emotional,
spiritual, financial, and physical needs.
One cares, respects, nurtures, and is consistently involved.

Shadows

Someone can love you
with every fiber of their being,

be the kind of person who
gives the proverbial shirt off their back.

They can be the beloved daughter, son, coworker, pastor,
and at the same damn time, be one of the most
oppressive, manipulative, destructive abusers
whose toxic behavior
stays hidden behind
silence,
secrets,
masking,
and their *good-enough* deeds.

You are *not* crazy.
You are *not* the problem.
It's their dysfunction.

Lowered Expectations

I've broken my own heart a thousand times.
I'm not breaking it anymore.

I HAD to learn to accept people at face value,
to understand that people don't change
simply because I want them to,
or because I understand
their trauma, *or* because
I see their potential.

I used to believe my prayers, positive intentions, and manifestations
could change a person,

that I could make them stop hurting me.
That I could make them see my heart.

While powerful, no prayers, intentions, or manifestations
are enough to change someone who is
committed to remaining abusive.

I had to learn to believe people
and their actions towards me.

I had to let go of the stories that I told myself,
the stories that I made up about them.
Stories that I created to make bad people appear human.

I had to stop believing the best in everybody.

I had to learn to not go around expecting
too much decency, humanity, and common sense.

Second Amendment

You know how at the zoo, when animals attack a human,
the policy states the animal must be put down?

How come we don't have similar laws for
people who kill innocent people?

If you take a life, you lose a life.

Nothing taken can be kept.

That should be the law.

Dear Oppressors,

I will not weaken myself so that you can become
stronger. May a swift death come to misogynoir,
patriarchy, white supremacy, and capitalism.

Busy People

Another app, another follow, another post,
another comment,
and all I really want is *connection*.

Another reel, another meme, another graphic,
another hashtag, another share,
and all I really want is *validation*.

Another retreat, another meetup, another group,
another registration,
another credit card charge, and all I really want is *community*.

Another gimmick, another tool, another idea,
another goal, another task,
and all I really want is to know that *my life matters* to you.

Another text, another WhatsApp, another Voxer,
another MarcoPolo, another DM
another Zoom, another Signal, another Facetime,
another Google Meet,
and all I really want is to spend time with you—in *real* life.

And to have brunch and stay in touch, to hug,
to have my family over for movie night,
to kiss my partner goodnight
and go on a romantic getaway.
To make plans with my girlfriends
and make memories with my loved ones.

It's the simple things...

Like getting to know my neighbors and waving to passersby.
To share freshly baked banana bread
and have a good conversation with a stranger.

I'm asking about your day, but
what I really want to know is
if you miss me the way that I miss you.

I'm asking about your weekend, but
what I really want to hear is
that you want to spend it with me.

Born to Serve

I thought of others more than of myself.
I gave much more than I took.
I said *yes* more than I said *no.*

I was present for others more than for myself.
I compromised more than I ever stated my limits.
I forgave others faster than I forgave myself.

I lied to protect their feelings.
I made excuses for others
more than I made space for my truth.

And that's how I lost *myself*...

When I detach from you,
am I doing what's *really* best for me?

Or...

Are my traumatized parts trying to circumvent future heartbreak?

Red Alert

If you *can't* feel my love and
I *can't* feel your love,
then we're bypassing each other
within the shadows
of our own fears.

I See You, Boo

No part of you wants to be visible
or vulnerable.

No part of you wants your truth exposed
much less be free.

Regret and shame run parallel through your veins.
Your jaw is too full of all the apologies
you were owed and never given.

It's a tragedy they made you believe you had to exist
this way.

I love you.

A little birdie asked me,
"Are you changing, or are you healing?"

I said,
"A person can change without ever being healed.
But you cannot heal without changing."

Finding Self-Esteem

Like the profiles
on those god-forsaken
dating apps,
I swipe left
on every opportunity to meet you.

I deny myself the gift of being in a relationship.
I tell myself that she is...
Too attractive.
Too beautiful.
Too intelligent.
Too professional.
Too spiritual.
Too put-together.
Too small.
Too healthy.
Too un-traumatized.
Too fashionable.

Too much
of everything I've always wanted.

And by the 614th swipe,

I realize
I am too immersed in the waters
of *not-enoughness*.

I need to work on myself, so that I can fully meet you.

I am enough.
I am enough.
I am enough.

For My Protection

Walls are so underrated.
My walls shield me,
hide me,
support me,
and shelter me.

They become a bridge for me.
Provide an exit for me,
and elevate me.

I love my walls.

List some ways that your walls protect you:

1. _____

2. _____

3. _____

4. _____

5. _____

Storage Needed

I wish that I could place my pain in a pretty little box.

Like hazardous waste in its own disposable container.

Categorized by lost love, disappointments,
traumas, and regrettable decisions.

Labeled:

TRIGGER WARNING
DO NOT TOUCH.
MAY CAUSE AN INTENSE EMOTIONAL REACTION

My body, mind, and spirit are too full
of what *doesn't* belong.

Like PPE, I use smiles, lying eyes, even denial
to protect myself from harm.

MASKING MANDATORY

Why can't hiding my pain be as antiquated
as old-school methods of storing important records?

Each event fitted onto the microfiche of my life story.

All of the foreign and familiar, broken into
sections: 1980s, 1990s, and 2000s.

Not even the Dewey Decimal System could help me
classify all the years of trauma.

I need a way to hide my pain.

I Spy

Two girls chasing each other through freshly cut grass.

One's wearing speckled pink and white Dora-the-Explorer pajamas

holding a bald, brown-eyed baby doll.
The other is wearing a simple peach and navy-blue short set.

They're barefoot.

I observe them

wishing to be barefoot, too.

They're unconcerned about danger

as they laugh and play.

I wish I could play, too,

and be like them:

free.

To run, jump, and flip

amongst the butterflies and the beauty

of just being born,

the epitome of joy.

No Time

A force field existed where love belonged.

No windows, no doors, no seams.

It's a miracle any light got in at all.

Repressed memories, protected feelings,

hidden thoughts, and fabricated emotions.

Disingenuous responses.

Who am I?

I don't know.

I packed my issues deep inside,

perfected the art of disguising,

and replaced them with a smile.

How am I doing?

Nobody knows.

No one is wiser to my defenses.

My past, my present, parts of my future...

the trauma

rests comfortably on an imaginary shelf.

I'll pick it up later and sift through it

when I have time.

Acceptance

Meet me where I am.

Don't try to rearrange or re-imagine who I *should* be.

Don't tell me I would look or be a better person *if*—

Goddess didn't create me to fit inside of your mold.

Given half the opportunity, you'd help me lose my identity.

I know I'm not like the others,

not who you thought I was when—

Anyway, love me because you *see* the real me.

Appreciate my qualities

because I'm different.

I Feel All the Feels

It hurts to be ghosted,
cheated on,
and ignored.

It hurts to be broken up with and rejected.
Abandoned.

It hurts to be betrayed,
lied to, and gossiped about.
To have my secrets shared.

I can't
fix it.
Nor can I defend myself
or get answers.

Maybe the pain of betrayal
will never go away. Not for a while.

Maybe I'll have a breakdown
before the breakthrough.

For now?

I'll breathe, rest, trust.

Maybe try again

soon.

Friends Now, Strangers Soon

You'll tell me
it's been *crazy busy*.
Life's been *lifin'*.
It's the kids,
partner,
COVID,
work,
hell, world issues.

But...
I know you're pulling away.
Dissociating.
Placing me at the bottom of your priority list.

I know the distance will only grow until we're no more,
until our friendship will become a distant memory,
with once-a-year texts.
Please don't place me there
while I figure out how to hold on to you, to us.

I miss you.

The Longest Distance

One minute, we're sister friends,
vacationing together,
laughing,
planning meals,
sharing the details of our lives,
and swearing each other to secrecy,

making memories that were supposed to last a lifetime...
Spending our birthdays together
and cackling over texts or making up acronyms.

Celebrating successes
and witnessing vulnerabilities.

Standing in the gap
for chosen sisters, friends, and queens.

In the words of Whitney, "Didn't we almost have it all?"
Tears flow as I remember that I always do this to myself.
Expecting too much, too soon, from far
too many.

I do it to myself.

For the first time, I felt like the cool kid in the clique
who found her people.

And now we don't talk anymore, and I don't know why.
But I miss you and wish you knew
how much I need you.

Black Women Only

When I'm around you,
I feel excited and nervous—like it's the first day of school.

Giddy over the possibility of making you my friend.
Sometimes, I fantasize about all the friend dates we'll plan.
All the secrets we'll share.
All the moments of laughter.

Will you be my friend?

I have to silence the parts of me that tell me:
I don't belong.
I'm not enough.
And inside... deep inside, I know I *am* enough,
and we *need* each other.

I love you, Black women.

Repeat these words to your younger self:

"I am so sorry for hurting you, for not believing you, for forgetting you.

I love you."

What Would You Tell Your Younger Self?

_____

_____

_____

_____

_____

_____

_____

_____

_____

_____

II.
Tending to the Wound

In my life, it became apparent that I had to choose me in ways I had never chosen me before.

Decision Point

What am I doing with the trauma?

Am I passing it on to others?

Holding onto it?

Am I stopping it?

Healing it?

What am I doing?

Phrases I Hate the Most

1. ***"I'm here for you."***
    You're not *here*—you're likely hundreds,
    even thousands of miles away.
    You're likely busy working, parenting
    your children, or hanging out with
    your in-person friends.
    I'm alone—you are not *here*.

    Alternatives: Would it be okay to check in
    later this week? Would a visit feel supportive?
    If you need to cry, shout, or sit in silence—I'm
    comfortable and can shoulder it. How about
    a phone call or a Zoom lunch date?

2. ***"I'm holding space for you."***
    Are you? Tell me how you're holding space for
    my grief, depression, and sadness. Where are you
    holding it? What are you going to do with it? If
    you're holding something on my behalf, why do I
    feel like I'm being swallowed up in my aloneness?

    Alternatives: I'm thinking about you.
    What would feel most supportive or loving
    to you? How can I show up for you?

3. ***"I'm sending you love and light."***
    How are you sending something that I *can't*
    feel? Do you have the right address?

    Alternatives: I love you.

    Instead of asking, "How are you doing?"

    Ask, "How can I help you with *the doing*?"

Affirmation

I let go and release all negative energy.
I forgive those who deserve my forgiveness.
I acknowledge I am not handcuffed to any human—
neither am I bonded
by their treatment or abuse of me.
I am free.

My healing journey started when I realized Goddess and I were on the same wavelength. She sees me as I have not been fully able to see myself, whole, healed, and beautiful. She wants the best for me. She loves every part of me.

In honor of D.G.

"To be a truth-teller,
you have to own the truth of who you are."

"Until you acknowledge your sacredness,
you cannot have your sacred boundaries."

"It is okay to see the goodness in people
and also protect yourself from people."

Parenting Self

It takes a lot more than egg and sperm
to earn the title of *parent*.

It takes a lot more than biology
to earn the title of *family*.

And where others have failed,
I now know I can create what I need.

Constant apologizing with no behavioral change is
some bullshit. ~**M.S.**

Affirmation:
I'm not too traumatized to be in a relationship
with a less traumatized person.
I'm deserving of healthy love. We traumatized people
deserve untraumatized people. ~**M.S.**

People who use too many categories and labels to define who they are scare me.

I honor my need to move and evolve with fluidity, curiosity, and mystery.

I won't be confined.

I Know Who I Am

I'm not introverted
or anti-social.

I'm not mean
or stuck-up.

I'm not shy, either.

I *am* selective.

Discerning.
Intuitive.
Protective.

I *am* centering my peace.

Communal Care

For far too long, I believed I could make it alone.

"I don't need anybody. Fuck 'em!"

But the truth is that I need love. It's the core
of my survival.
I am nothing without love. I am nothing
without my community of beautiful, kindred souls.

I am *everything* with them and *nothing* without them.

There is no forward progress without *my* people.
There is no self-care, soul-care, or community care
without *my* people.

"Love me now, or I'll go crazy." ~ **Chaka Khan (*Sweet Thing*)**

The Polarity of Our Love

I feel your
arousal and suppression,
warmth and coldness,
passion and apathy,
freedom and confinement,
safety and danger,
intimacy and separation,
endurance and impermanence,
understanding and confusion,
transparency and secrecy.

I just want you to know I love you.

Divine Connection

The fear of the goddess
is the beginning of
ignorance,
insecurity, even
shame.

Love diminishes fear.

The love of the goddess within you
is the beginning of wisdom,
intuition,
connection,
self-love, and
courage.

Together, Healing

I want to see you empowered.
I want you to see me empowered.

I want to see you healed.
I want you to see me healed.

I want to see you living in abundance.
I want you to see me living in abundance.

May we become co-conspirators
on our quest toward freedom.

Dead On Arrival

Do you *know* how many things tried to kill me?

Summer 1979: Transported to planet Earth
via 18-year-old *Death Mother*.
Instead of feeding me milk from her bosom,
she injected me
with rage, resentment, and unwantedness.

Father? Missing in Action

Spring/Summer 1987: The person introduced as *"sibling"*
violently touched my body with his adolescent hands.

February 2001: I turned being unwanted onto myself
and tried to take my life,
Method? A bullet to brokenness.
Rest in peace, mind, body, and spirit.

The universe said, "It's not my time to leave."

I am not afraid or intimidated by *anyone's* judgment
of me. I survived for reasons you will never understand.

Make a decision today that scares the shit out of you.
What scares you? List them here:

1. _____

2. _____

3. _____

4. _____

5. _____

6. _____

7. _____

8. _____

9. _____

10. _____

I want to be the biggest red flag
to the wrong kind of people.

Affirmation: I have true friends who just haven't met me yet.

Baby Steps

Ignoring the wound,
wishing it away,
speaking harshly about it
and hating it
won't make it heal
any faster.

So try something different.

Tend to the wound.
Acknowledge it.
Listen to it.
Write about it.
Talk about it.
Draw a timeline,
reflecting on each wound (who, what, when, where).
Hold your wound story
securely
compassionately.

Tend to it.

Other People's Pain

We were never supposed to
turn numb
and apathetic,
closing our eyes
to the suffering of
one another.

Return to love.
Return to humanity.
Return to
community.

That Pride Kinda Love

Love is love,
rejection is not.

Love is love,
discrimination and *prejudice* are not.

Love is love,
racism is not.

Love is love,
bigotry is not.

Love is love,
oppression is not.

Love is love,
control and *manipulation* are not.

Love is love,
disrespect is not.

Love is love,
selfishness is not.

Love is love,
abuse is not.

Love is love,
fear is not.

Love is love,
abandonment is not.

Love is love,
intimidation is not.
Love is love.
Love is... *Love.*

My body is not a vessel for holding trauma.
It deserves relief.

Beloved,

Your precious heart
will feel like it's going to burst.

You will feel like you can't
go on,
like you'll never recover from
the pain they caused.

But you can.
You fucking *CAN*.

I love you.

Permission to Unravel

Do *not*
for one second
feel ashamed or regretful over the unraveling,

for becoming undone or
for breaking down those titanium walls.
Walls, that, for a long time, served
as the illusion of protection
you believed would keep you intact.

The walls that would prevent you from getting hurt,
keep friends from judging you,
keep lovers from mishandling
the most tender parts of you.

The unraveling has opened your eyes,
allowing you to speak your truth and
make decisions in your best interests.

It has kept you honest and courageous.
It made you *real*, even human.

Do you see it now?

How those titanium walls
kept out the truth *and* prevented
real and lasting love from entering?

How they've kept you from meeting yourself?

Do not despise the unraveling.
It created a path for
new beginnings, new stories,
new love, and a new future.

Unraveling is, at times, the only way
to meet your truth.

True Strength

I've reached a point in my life
Where I'm less concerned
about keeping up with the *myth*
of strength.

The truth is, I'm strong.
But I'm not *that* strong.
I cannot and will not withstand every storm.
I can't endure *everything*.

I'm breakable.

When I'm cut, I bleed.

Nor can I do *everything*
that I put my mind to, either.

I need help. I need people.

Sometimes, I'm going to cry.
Other times, I'm going to give up.
And that's okay—reaching my breaking point
reminds me that I have limits.

We *all* do.
I'm not that strong and neither are you.

What you call *strength,*
I call, "having no other choice."

I'm no longer pretending to be stronger than I am.
I'm no longer suppressing my pain, grief, sadness,
frustration, worry, or anger.

As long as I live, truth and vulnerability
will be my new version of *strong*.

It takes time to step into your *enoughness*.

Common Sense

Mistakes will be made.
It's inevitable.
I'm not supposed to know
anything that I have never
been taught.

Affirmation:
I am teachable and ready to learn
how to become the best version of myself.

On Healing

Some people will reject the person you are becoming.
A swift, painful dismissal from your life.

There will be moments
when you feel pressured
to cling
to the old and familiar,
the known and safe,
even when it hurts.

This is only a part of the process, but it isn't the end.

Healing will always require you
to purge, let go, change directions,
and ease into a new
and uncharted territory.

So...
allow them to leave.
Give yourself permission
to fall apart,
to grieve,
to heal.

Knowing that one day,
life won't remain this hard
and relationships won't be this messy.

Healthy is on the way.

Trying

I'm trying
to live in the best way that I can,

to keep my eyes on who and what's important,

on where my body feels safe,
and how I can stay present enough
to relax,
to feel pleasure.

I'm trying to live,
to make the most of life.
One that I didn't choose but that chose me.

I'm trying to figure out
how to leave a legacy,
live peacefully,
and locate happiness.

I'm trying.
So let me live.

Q: What are you doing?

A: Everything. I'm doing *everything*, so
don't come here wasting my time.

I Can't Hear You

If you don't want to...?
Say so.

If you can't...?
Say so.

If you're not interested anymore...?
Say so.

If you don't know what to say...?
Say so.

If you don't have the money...?
Say so.

If you don't have the time...?
Say so.

If you've changed your mind...?
Say so.

If your energy has shifted...?
Say so.

If you're afraid...?
Say so.

If you're doubting...?
Say so.

But don't fucking ghost me. I know the names
of every person in my life.
My body has a space reserved just for you.
So when you get silent or get weird,
my body revolts and anger builds.

Speak UP instead of ghosting.

Let It Be

Parentified adult children are tired.
Our backs hurt from carrying the weight
of those who didn't have the parental skills
necessary to raise us.
Our spines are in pain from growing
backbones too early in life
because the adults around us didn't use theirs.

We're emotionally and physically exhausted
from figuring everything out,
making adult decisions,
caring for adult emotions, and prioritizing
the adults above ourselves.
We had to *BE* the emotional stability
and safety *we* needed the most.
To my parentified community,
bless the exhaustion.

Bless the anger and the rage, too.
Bless the need for rest, quiet, and peace.
Bless the needs as well as the wants.
Bless the support that you deserve
and are afraid to ask for.

Bless it—*don't* fight it.

Bless it—*don't* avoid it.
Bless it, and let it be.

Wrong Connection

I've learned
to not trust anyone who wants to take care of me
more than they take care of themselves.
The people who swear they love me
more than they love themselves.

In the words of RuPaul, "How you gonna love me
when you don't love yourself...?"

When Everything Isn't Enough

We gave all that we had,
until there was nothing left.

I gave you *everything*,
except what mattered most,
my heart.

You gave me *everything*
except what mattered most,
your respect and trust.

I'm so sorry.

In My Body

I didn't feel anything.
I didn't feel
a thing.
And then, I did...
But I didn't know how to start living.

I only knew how to stay close
to the story of my trauma.

But now,
I'm feeling everything.
Now,
I'm laughing.
Now I am back home
in my body.

Thank you.

You were trying to take care of me.
I was trying to take care of you.
We didn't know how to truly take care of ourselves.

Life Lessons Last Forever

I'm still learning that...
I can tell the truth without being punished.

I'm still learning
how to communicate
my needs.

I'm still learning
how to process
discomfort without leaning into the urge to vacate
people, places, and opportunities.

I'm still learning
the differences between fear, intuition, and my voice.

I'm still learning
that it's better to disappoint others than to live
with regret.

I'm still learning
how to surrender instead of control.

I'm still learning
that I can be
better, bigger, and more.

I'm still learning
that my life has value.

I'm still learning how to love myself.

Too Much, Too Many

I'm at the point in my life
where I don't want to forgive too many things
or pretend to be okay with how
their actions impacted me mentally, emotionally,
spiritually, and physically.

I'm only human, after all.

I'm at the point in my life where the wounds
won't disappear
as quickly as they used to.
Where the parts of me that used to pretend
to not be hurt, to be okay, to forgive and move on—
those parts are hungry for justice.

I'm at the point in my life where I
immediately notice when energy changes.
I can feel when someone is about to ghost me.

I'm at the point in my life
where everything matters.
Everything is felt.
Everything is a big deal.
Everything needs to be discussed,
worked out,
and processed.

There's too much silence,
too much manipulation,
passivity,
and conflict.

Too many broken promises,
and too much assuming that I'll be okay
after you hurt me.

The Journey

I can't afford
to spend too much time
thinking about
the ones who hurt me.

I can't.

I've gotta
make up for lost time,
and make up for all the moments
I wasn't loved.
Wasn't respected.
Wasn't thought of.
Wasn't treated as
the precious one that I am.

I'm gonna spend the rest of my life
prioritizing *me*.
Loving *me*.
Listening to *me*.
Keeping *me* safe.

There's no more time to lose.
I'm just over here, busy learning how
to love *me*.

When someone tries to convince you
that all you've ever been
is all you'll ever be?
Prove them wrong.

Answer these questions:

1.   Who are you?

_____

2.   Who do people expect you to be?

_____

3.   Who do you feel that you should be?

_____

4.   Who are you aspiring to be?

_____

5.   What is one action you have taken or
       will take towards your becoming?

_____

Trauma may have laid the
foundation for my healing journey,
but it cannot sustain me...

It has destabilized me long enough.

Royalty

I learned how
to become what other people wanted
from an early age.

I learned how
to be liked.
Desired.
Chosen.

I learned how
to be attractive.
Smart.
Needed.
Domesticated.

To serve
and put others first.

I am not a servant, helpmate, or submissive partner.

Call me *Queen*.

Beware
of those who
try to tell you
who you are
when they don't
even know themselves.

No matter how you present yourself to the world,
your sexuality, gender, presence,
your true self—just as you are—
is beloved.

**When they don't add to my life,
I subtract their presence from my life.**

Self

I gave you all
my love, time,
even my best years.

I didn't know
I needed to save something
for myself.

Now, I'm pouring everything,
everything, into me.

Yes, I Can

I can love others
and hold them accountable.

I can respect my family of origin
and still hold them accountable.

I can value my relationships
and still hold them accountable.

I can forgive
and still hold them accountable.

Accountability is an essential part
of having healthy, loving relationships.

May you know the kind of safety that allows you the freedom to no longer carry the burden of your secrets.

On Being a Safe Person to Survivors

- Courageously, explicitly name the pain, name the wrongness *out loud*.
- Take sides with the survivor *in front of the abuser* and the abuser's supporters.
- Listen and validate repeatedly—*never tire of hearing about the trauma you didn't experience.*
- Treat the harm and trauma as if it's the worst incident to transpire in the survivor's life, *because it probably is.*
- Refrain from creating a story about why the abuser committed the offense and why they need to be forgiven.
- *Seek justice and accountability* on behalf of the survivor before sharing any tidbits of wisdom on the necessity to forgive.
- Help the survivor establish boundaries, autonomy, and safety—*may your presence be their shield.*
- Keep everything confidential and seek permission from the survivor before sharing their painfully vulnerable experiences.

Just for Today

Take a break.

Take items *off* your to-do list.

Take a friend's call.

Take a minute to show gratitude.

Take people, places, and things that no longer serve you *off* your schedule.

Take your health seriously.

Take a few deep breaths.

Take a sip of water.

Take care of your body.

Take a moment to show love for yourself and others.

Take time to forgive yourself for decisions you made when you had no other options.

Take time to reflect on your journey.

Affirmation: If I can be one within, I will not be at war with others.

Gratitude

Gratitude is less about having a ritual of appreciation
and more about
remembering the answered prayers,
innate gifts,
opportunities,
surprises,
lessons learned,
community,
love,
nature,
health and healing,
privilege,
the ebbs and flows,
and the ease and refreshment.

Queer and Loved
June 4th, 2023

My queer self
is less about the rainbows,
performative allyship, and cliché phrases,
and more about the realization that

someone somewhere is
being denied friendship and family
because of their sexual orientation or gender identity.

They feel stuck in a pattern of identity-masking
due to internalized phobias.
They're terrified of being outed,
and afraid to question or explore their curiosity
because it may mean the loss
of their job, family, or community.

They've decided to remain
the gender assigned at birth because they believe
it will make life easier for others.

They're convinced they must remain celibate
or else face a disapproving God and go to hell.

They're being beaten, imprisoned,
and sentenced to death.
 Or they've ended their life due to being unloved
and unprotected.

I'm going to love myself and love people
who share my queer identity.
Defining myself *for myself* is a powerful
and meaningful action that I take
against white supremacy.

Your Queerness Matters If:

You kissed a person of the same sex or gender one time
and liked it but felt
ashamed and afraid afterward.

You had same-sex/gender encounters
during early childhood and were made to feel
wrong or dirty.

You secretly fantasize about being intimate
with a person of the same sex/gender.

You're publicly against LGBTQ+ relationships,
but watch them in pornography.

You listened to a homophobic or transphobic sermon
on Sunday but are questioning your own identity.

You questioned your sexuality
or had brief encounters in the past
but never told your spouse.

You are in a heteronormative relationship
but secretly get turned on when seeing queer couples.

You told your child they would be disowned
or face eternal damnation if they were LGBTQ+,
but keep your own past a secret.

You speak out against the LGBTQ+ community
but are secretly wishing you could explore
your curiosities.

You were raised in a home
where being anything other than hetero
and cis-gendered was shunned, so every decision
you made was based out of the fear of God,
fear of alienation, fear of judgment,
or a deep desire to please.

You never got the chance to live
on your own terms, and you regret that.

Happy Pride to you. I hope you find yourself
and get free.

Mothered

I would have avoided
a lot of failed relationships
and heartbreak
if someone had taught me:

In case of emergency,
scream to the top of my lungs
until someone hears me.

Set standards.

Hold boundaries.

Being needed is not the same thing as being loved.

How to say "no" often.

How to communicate my wants and needs.

How to respond to disrespect.

How to listen and honor my intuition.

How to connect, become emotionally healthy,
and identify the same in others.

How to play and incorporate pleasure
as a life ritual.

How to become more comfortable
with silence and stillness.

How to spend time with plants and animals.

Lowered Expectations

I don't expect too much out of people.
I expect good people to mostly go about doing good shit.

I expect not-so-good people to mostly do terrible shit.

I keep expectations of myself manageable,
giving myself a lot of grace.
That way, I'm not floating in a sea
of disappointment and despair.

I've had to learn not to expect too much
out of anyone but myself.

Helpless

Since AI is so popular and can do almost anything,
can it do things humans *can't* do?

Can it stop gun violence?
How about war?

Can it stop terrorism?
Genocide?

Can it stop sexual assault?
Maybe save endangered species?

Can it stop children from being abused?
How about white supremacy?

Can AI solve real-world problems?

Privilege?

I read something recently that said,
"It's a privilege to be alive, be grateful."

But I'd like to counter this cliché and obtuse point.
It's not much of a *privilege* if it hurts.

It's not a privilege for those who live in fear
of being murdered or for those who are unemployed
and financially insecure.

It's not a privilege for people who don't have
food, clothing, shelter, clean water, or clean air.

It's not a privilege for people who experience
violence, war, or terrorism.

It's not a privilege for people who live without
being loved, cared for, and supported,
or for those who exist
with survivor's remorse and overwhelming grief.

It's not a privilege for people who live
with chronic, agonizing, or debilitating medical diagnoses.

Privilege for one *isn't* privilege for all.

Many people are born into privilege,
while others are born into hardship.
Some people have hard days, while others
have hard lives.

Part of being a good human means
showing compassion and understanding
for other people and *their* experiences.

Identity

I've learned I can't depend on whiteness
to tell me who I am or should become.
I had to find out for myself.

My Black-ass truth is enough.
My Black ass body is enough.
My Black-ass wisdom is enough.

**It's okay to feel out loud even though we live in a
world that prefers we keep our feelings inside.**

To read out loud:

The right energy will gravitate towards me.
The right opportunities will come at the right time.
The right people will love me.
The right jobs will hire me.
The right words will be spoken by me.

I will accept *nothing* less.

Reader, this is an invitation to write five
manifestations for your future.

List them here:

You Only Live Once (YOLO)

Sometimes, the people in our lives
will criticize our decisions
because they see courage
and a level of tenacity in us that they've never
possessed for themselves.

Your preparation, drive, intention-setting, and action
triggers jealousy masked
as anger, judgment, resentment, sadness, and grief.

So...

Buy the house.
Accept the job.
Have the child,
or live child-free.

Get the degree.
Come out.
Start the relationship.
Date how *and* who you want,
or honor your singleness.

Relocate.
Write the book.
Create the workshop.
Change that hairstyle and
wear what you want.

Get the tattoo
and the piercing.
Love your body—at *every* size.
Do whatever *you* want.

Meditation

My body is my temple. It belongs to me.
The abuse of my body doesn't define me.
It's what happened *to* me.
It's *not* me.

I have a right to receive and give pleasure.
I'm allowed to express my feelings
in whatever way feels safe.
I have a choice in how I give and receive sexual pleasure.
I can say *no*. I can say *yes*.

I'm allowed to be vulnerable.
I'm allowed to explore and experiment.
I'm allowed to be curious
as well as present and alive.
I'm allowed to take control *and* submit control.
It's *my* choice.
I'm grateful for a responsive body, mind, and soul.
I'm allowed to climax.
I am beautiful.

I am regaining my strength.
I am using my voice.

I am allowed to verbalize my needs and desires.
I can say, *give me more*.
I can say, *stop*.
I can feel trauma exiting my body.
I can feel toxic energy exiting my body.
I can feel my body healing.

Courage Becomes Her

Looking back,
I realize each time I trusted in
someone else's vision for my life
over my own
I lost a piece of my Self.
Each time I prioritized someone else's
emotional stability and wellness
over my own,
I lost connection to what made me
feel, think, & have clarity.
Each time I relied on someone else
to fulfill me or make me whole,
I became more depressed,
anxious,
hopeless,
unsure of myself,
Each time I adopted someone else's fears,
making them my own,
courage
quietly walked
out of the door.

Well, here's to returning to Self.

Familiarity

So often, we replicate what is most familiar.
Silence when shit hits the fan.
The canary in the coal mine must be the issue,
instead of the reason the canary sings.
Losing weight trumps shedding toxic family patterns.
Addiction to the over-consumption
of material items or over-performing.
God is Man. Man is God.
What's the purpose of women, then?
To serve and leave *nothing* for herself?

What are the thoughts, feelings, beliefs, and practices that have made a home within you?

List Them Here:

- _____

- _____

- _____

- _____

- _____

Matthew Chapter 25

If we're going to start a war,
it should be one with a mission to destroy
white supremacy.
One that gives voice to the voiceless
and is committed to ending human suffering.

We should all pledge allegiance
to equality, healthcare, climate change,
education, and mental health reform.

We should be committed to
building relationship bridges.

Not walls.

NO MORE racism, sexism, xenophobia,
greed, queerphobia, or bigotry.

NO MORE terrorism, genocide, child abuse, or poverty.

May we heal this sick world.
To the least of...
Let us clothe, feed, comfort, heal, sacrifice, donate,
and HELP.

Not hurt.
Let us protect, honor, fight for, and listen to others.

May we exercise our right
to love, hug, serve, and encourage one another.

May we build weapons of mass
understanding, respect, civility, and peace.

May we stand our ground
to address system oppression and disenfranchisement.

If we are going to fight, let it be for the least of...

Just for today, love yourself by *stopping* any asshole who tries to treat you poorly.

For Adult Children Who Remain Silent

I used to swallow my feelings
wishing them away
so they wouldn't
get in the
way.

For the sake of protecting your image and
protecting your feelings.

For the sake of protecting myself from abandonment
and for the sake of survival.

I'm exhausted from protecting you
more than protecting myself.

Toxic Relatives

They thought I would die with their secrets.
They assumed I would forget about
what they did to me
and others.

Like so many times before,
they didn't know
I would one day regain my power.

Self-Leadership

Intuition is power.
Why else would oppressors and power hoarders
condition us to ignore it?

It's rarely the case
that we don't know what to do.
It's that we're afraid of failure.
Afraid of the unknown.
Afraid of the opinions of those closest to us.
Afraid of trusting our own process.
Ask Intuition to make her-*self* known.

When one person speaks up?
Stand with them.
Guard them.
Comfort them.
Publicly support them.
As it may be an opportunity
for you to speak up, too,
and start a revolution.

Middle Age Questions

What if the mid-life crisis isn't a *crisis* at all,
but an unraveling of your antiquated self?
A re-emerging of your authentic self?

What if
the midlife crisis
was created to keep people ashamed
of wanting more?
Of seeking freedom?

What if
the mid-life crisis
is bullshit?

Choose Real Love

Love and commitment
can change
because we are
ever-changing and
ever-evolving.

Love will never ask you to remain
on a sinking ship.

Love will never require that you remain
in misery.

Love will never ask you to sacrifice
your health, your purpose, or your autonomy.

Love will never ask you to stay
when it hurts
or when it's killing you.

Choose to love yourself today.

I can have compassion for the trauma
my abusers experienced and *STILL*

have enough compassion for myself to:
Leave dysfunctional relationships.
Create healthy boundaries.
End all forms of disrespect.
Make decisions that are in my best interest.

Practice Saying...

No.
Not today and
probably not tomorrow.
Maybe never.
I don't want to.
I can't.
I'm tired.
I have limited capacity.
I have zero capacity.
Life is *lifing*.
My energy level conflicts with your request.
I've changed my mind.
My availability has shifted.
It's not a good time.
I'll think about it.
I'm not the right fit.
Intuitively speaking, this doesn't feel right.
My ancestors told me to say, "no."

Finding You

I don't have to be everything,
do everything, or
know everything.

But if I don't know anything else,
I know myself.
I know what I believe.
I know what gives me joy.
I know where I feel the most at peace.
I know my truth.

Find yourself.
Find yourself.
Find *yourself*.

There is nothing more precious
than your time, energy, voice,
words, and presence.
Use all of it in ways that honor
your inherent self-worth.
Share it with people who
reciprocate and appreciate.

Capitalism Kills

You don't have to chase everything that runs.

What's hot today will be stale tomorrow.

You don't have to chase trends
to remain relevant, either.

Rest.

Stillness is a gift. Use it wisely.

Anxiety

The angst I'm feeling
to pick up the phone, scroll, reply, refresh,
follow, search, shop, or scroll some more...

That's called anxiety, distraction, procrastination,
boredom, disconnection, or addiction.

Stillness is a gift.

May I rest so that my soul can speak.

Truth-Teller Trauma

It's not that we don't want family around—
we don't want to be treated as enemies.
It's not that we enjoy being estranged, either.
We left so that we could learn to love ourselves.
It's being ostracized in places
where we were supposed to be protected.
It's that you punished us
for simply responding to your dysfunction.
It's not being able to make the dysfunction *functional*.
The unlovable *lovable*.
The inconsistent *consistent*.
The unsafe *safe*.
It's how we've always had to stand alone in acknowledging our pain.
It's all that has been left unsaid,
especially the apologies we'll never hear.
It's that we will spend the rest of our lives grieving
what we will never have.
It's that 10/10 times, *we're* the ones
required to forgive, forget, and move on.
It's that 10/10 times, we're not validated,
supported, respected, or comforted.
Instead, we're dismissed, forgotten, intentionally
misunderstood, and neglected.
It's the way we spend our lives
self-soothing and being self-reliant.
It's how family members have chosen their fear
over our safety, justice, and advocacy.

One Life

In the end, I will remember all the roles
I tried to fill to make others accept me.

All the times I abandoned myself.

All the times I was quiet
when I should have spoken up.

All the times I said *yes*
when I should have said *no*.

All the opportunities, relationships, and experiences
I missed because of fear.

Nothing Wasted

Goddess, would you make something
beautiful from what remains
of the remnants of my trauma?

The parts of me that feel
more like a hollow void that whispers,
"Tell me where it hurts."
I whisper back, "I don't know... It's too much."

Would you make something beautiful
from my fears, questions, doubts, and all this rage?
None of what I went through was worth it,
but please make something beautiful
out of what remains.

Funny-style Frenemies

Life is too short to keep people in your life
who carry "funny-style" energy
that makes you feel uncomfortable,

unsafe, or like you can't trust them.
I don't think we realize that our threshold
for discomfort, weird shit,
or unnecessary emotional labor is super low right now.

So please don't act surprised if a relationship
has changed recently due to:

1. **Boundary concerns**
2. **Thoughtless comments**
3. **Feeling unsafe or uncomfortable**
4. **Unspoken or unresolved harm**
5. **Trauma or drama dumping**
6. **Feeling unheard**
7. **Too many unexplained silences or absences**
8. **Unreciprocated care and support**
9. **Dishonesty**
10. **Disrespect**

**Some relationships deserve repair,
while others deserve dissolution.**

Growing Pains

When you start changing or
rearranging your schedule,
making choices that mirror
your wants, needs, desires—

They'll say *you're crazy.*
That *you've changed.*
You're avoidant.
You're distant.

That they don't know you anymore.
They don't know what happened to you.
You must be going through some
existential crisis,
and maybe you are.
Or
maybe, just maybe,
you've come to the realization
that you no longer need to live your life
for other people.

You're on the right track. Keep going.

Go to Therapy

Because of therapy,
I love myself fully and completely.
I no longer disparage my body.
I don't question my life purpose or place in the world.
I don't let assholes treat me poorly.

I know how to speak up for myself.
I recognize and trust my intuition.
I know the difference
between being stuck and being afraid.
I can make decisions that scare me.
I can feel my feelings without using
people and hobbies to distract me.
I can feel my feelings without fear
of being overwhelmed by them.
I can ask for what I need.

I respect my complexities and contradictions.
I allow myself to cry privately and in front of others.
I love others deeply.
I trust myself.
I recognize those who have earned my trust.
I dream of a more beautiful future for myself.

I rest and allow ease.
I forgive myself.
I am honest about my pain.
My secrets don't control me.
Because of therapy,
I am leaving a legacy of warmth, tenderness, and healing.

Just for today, don't allow people to make you feel _okay_ about things that are very much _NOT OKAY_.

Write about a personal experience that is _very much not okay_:

_____

_____

_____

_____

_____

_____

_____

_____

_____

_____

_____

_____

_____

_____

My Friend,

The truth about healing
is that there is no real shortcut. Hard things
must be remembered, spoken, felt, and filtered
through the stories we create
so that we can locate the truth.

A major part of creating a *soft life*
is practicing being softer with yourself.
You'll have to intentionally choose
yourself over and over again.
You'll have to grieve people who choose
to remain unhealed and unchanged.

You will have to make space between yourself
and the people who harmed you
so that you don't prioritize their comfort
over your healing.

You'll have to practice honesty,
even when it hurts. No amount of healing
can change the past. Your future
depends on *you* being the change, the love,
and the support
you have always needed and deserved.

You will have to disappoint people
on the road to becoming unburdened.
You deserve all that you've always wanted
and never received.

I love you.

Q: How do we heal?
A: Individually and together

The process:

I sit with my ego, noticing when it gets in the way.
You can sit with yours, too.

I shine a light on my shadow and name the secret things.
You can do the same.

I acknowledge the ways that my trauma wounds
complicate relationships.
You can acknowledge yours, too.

I re-evaluate what I've been taught
to believe and what still rings true.
You can do it, too. We can always
unlearn and relearn.

I pay attention when I'm projecting,
manipulating, or exhibiting transference.
You can do the same.

I practice having scary, vulnerable,
and hard conversations.

You can meet me there. We can be afraid
together and make the hard things
easier.

I create goals for myself and a plan to reach them.
You can focus your attention on your goals, too.

I balance safety, love, and respect
for myself, and *then* I extend to others
what comes from my true *Self*.
We heal individually and then together.

This is how we heal, and this is how we grow.
This is how we practice liberative and embodied love.
Drink this
truth.
None of what happened was worth it.

None of what happened to you
is evidence of your value.

How do you quantify or qualify trauma?
What happened to you at the hands of others
could have *and* should have been prevented.

You don't have to carry the evidence
of their dysfunction.
Let me help you to let it go.

I love you.

Meditation Moment

Consider for a moment you are creating
the most loving future for yourself.
Think only of *you* right now.

What intentions would you set for yourself?
What kind of decisions would you make for your life?

What would be different?
What would end?
What would stay the same?

When you think about living
this imagined life, what comes up?
What sensations are you noticing in your body?
What kinds of emotions are being stirred?

What comes up for you after reading this meditation? Jot your notes here:

_____

_____

_____

_____

_____

_____

_____

_____

_____

_____

_____

_____

_____

_____

III.
Healing the Wound

The Wound

Tell me where it hurts.
How about here, in your chest? Maybe deep in your hips?

Show me how to love you.
With my arms? My words?
Show me how to take care of you when you're sick.
Whisper your love language.

Together, we'll draw a map
or paint a picture
of every wound
that longs to be healed.

Is it a gash? Sore? Fracture? A Judas kiss?

Let me be near.
Share your burdens.
Remind you that you
are finally safe
after all these years.

Tell me where it hurts,
so that I can inject love into all the places
that others have missed.

To Bub

You were and still are easy to love.
We grew up together.
We built a beautiful, full life.
We were Black and Beautiful.

You made me laugh.
You made me feel seen.
You protected me.
Countless times, you saved me.
You were there when I had nothing
but a name that I hated.

You were there.
You are still here, loving me through all the changes.
You healed the wounds
from every person who came before.
You encouraged me, pushed me, lifted me,
and stood toe-to-toe with me.

You made me a mother, daughter, friend...
For the rest of my life, I will love you.
You made me feel like I was the most important
person in the world.
And for these reasons and more, I will forever
love you. I will forever be there for you,
just like you have been for me.

Who Am I?
Tasha 7.9.2023

Lover, lesbian, Leo
a walking contradiction—
mother, sister, friend,
storyteller, truthteller, powerful manifester,
healer, dreamer, word weaver, believer,
serious about healing and purpose,
explorer of the goddess within us—
determination
rage
compassion
infectious laughter
hunger
passion
childlike wonder
creative
rebellious
learning to live for the first time in my life.

The Privilege

My ancestors spent their whole lives fighting.
I've spent my whole life fighting
for survival, too.

I'm not fighting anymore.
Peace is my shield and my compass.

M

Chosen is Better

My family didn't love me.
Didn't treat me right.
I created a new one, and I hope you do, too.

Owning my story gave me the right to change my story.

In the section below, I invite you to write about your own story. What would you like to remember? What would you like to keep? What would you like to change?

_____

_____

_____

_____

_____

_____

_____

_____

_____

_____

_____

You are allowed to hold the dualities of being human.
To be as complex as you are contradictory.
It takes as long as it takes to be the person
you've always wanted and to have the people
and resources you desire.

You are allowed to choose your own path to joy.
There will be pain that we cannot escape.
But nine times out of ten, you will survive.

I love you.

Proud of You

It takes a lot of courage
to go to therapy.

To allow the darkness
to come to light.

To reveal what has for so long
been the unspoken, hidden taboo.

To name what you were previously told
to keep secret.

It takes a lot of courage
to admit that you're not okay.

That you've been masking, shrinking,
and remaining silent
in order
to survive,
maintain relationships,
keep the agreement,
or be a good child, sibling, friend, and employee.
It takes a lot of courage
to prioritize yourself,
to find yourself,
to question,
to be curious,
and seek after that which will lead you
to your own enlightenment.

It takes a lot of courage
to admit your wrongs,
to make amends and repair,
and to ignore the critics.

It takes a lot of courage
to walk away,
to end the relationship,
to change,
speak up, and
challenge.

It takes a lot of courage
to keep living,
striving,
healing, and
growing.

I'm so damn proud of you.

When you think about yourself, what are you most proud of?

_____

_____

_____

_____

_____

_____

_____

_____

_____

_____

_____

_____

_____

_____

Valley Experiences

There are
hard days,
hard seasons,
and hard years.

You have what it takes
to get through them all.

But you can't do it by yourself.

No

Once you
make a decision for yourself,
establish the parameters,
regarding what you will and will not accept,
and decide that you need to honor
your intuition, and realize that you deserve
more, different, and better...

Once you choose *you*,
you'll be presented with a lot of chances
to do the opposite, to do the thing
you've always done.

Each opportunity is sent by the universe
to help you move in the direction of the life you desire.

Each opportunity is a practice in courage.
Each opportunity offers a chance
to strengthen that "no" muscle.

Beloved,

Sometimes someone not loving you
has nothing to do with you. Have you noticed
the way they treat themselves? Now pay close
attention to the ways they treat you, their criticism,
ice-cold demeanor, selfishness,
lack of acknowledgement of wrongdoing,
lack of heartfelt apology,
and lack of reciprocity.

If we allow truth to be witnessed,
people will tell us in a number of ways
that they're unable or unwilling
to love us in the way we need to be loved.

Listen carefully!

Do not reject the truth that's nestled
between their unloving-ness. Do not replace
their truth with the image you've created of them.
Do not hide the truth
behind the fantasy you've created.

Accept their truth, and go heal yourself. I love you.

What I want wants me, too.

At the end of my life, I will celebrate knowing that I
dared to live, summoned the determination to find
joy, *and* the courage to love and be loved.
And that I was brave enough to remember the parts
of my story that begged to be forgotten.

What are your deepest desires? List them here:

_____

_____

_____

_____

_____

_____

_____

_____

_____

_____

_____

_____

_____

_____

Self-Pleasure

Love yourself
slowly, passionately, intentionally.

Whisper sweet nothings
to your heart and
to your body.

Let all the previous versions
of yourself know
how beautiful and amazing you are.

Look at yourself
in the mirror. Be in awe of your
inner beauty,
intellect, smile, and
resolve.

Touch yourself
in all the places
that are starved
for affection and attention.

Self-pleasure *is* self-healing.

Make promises to yourself
that you're going to keep.

Spend time engaging
in activities that excite you.

Spend time with people
who connect you
to loving yourself
more and deeper.

I

Where Our Journey Ends

It's pruning season,
and I'm too far into my healing journey
to be in ambiguous relationships.

If I don't know where I stand with you...
If I don't know if you're a friend or not...
If I can't tell if we're still family or not...
If I can't detect whether the love is real...

I'm exiting the relationship.

Creating Joy

I'm trying
to be the change, so I can
make the best of this life.
To survive.
To live.

I worry that I don't have
a lot of time left,
and I'm trying to make sure
I don't waste
what I've been gifted.

I'm hoping that one day
I won't have to labor this hard,
and I can rest more.
Do more of what makes me
feel whole.

Love Starts with You

When I ask people about love,
I often hear,
"I don't know how to love myself."

Think of at least one person whose love
you melted into without question.
Think of how they loved you.
Think of how comforting and safe and sure it felt.

How did they let you know that they loved you?
Now, give that to yourself.

Gimmicks

My trauma isn't for profit.
It's not some get-rich-quick scheme.
It's not a marketing hack.
There is no fast track through trauma.
There are no real ten steps to freedom.
There is no sixty days to better self-esteem.
There is no such thing as thirty days to heal, either.

Healing can't happen from microwave methods.
Microwave methods are a marketing strategy.
Marketing strategies are a key component of capitalism.
Capitalism is a sibling of white supremacy.
White supremacy *doesn't* care about your trauma.

**Today I'm reminding myself
that the key to my liberation
belongs to me, and it's within my reach.**

Your First, Your Last

Do not wear this love,
our love,
as an accessory.

I am the
main drag,
the capsule,
the everyday tee,
the go-to,
the essential.

Act accordingly.

**You don't have to hate them to end the relationship.
You don't have to hate them to heal.
You don't have to hate them to choose yourself.**

More to Life

There's more to life than being needed,
being an essential employee,
having perfect attendance,
being the glue that holds the family together,
being the healer,
giving them everything they need,
and more than they deserve...

I wanted more.
I need
the most.
May I be
considered.
Respected. Desired. Cherished.
Accepted. Embraced. Celebrated. Loved.

Ease

I am tired of living
in the chaos,
high stress, and
crisis
of these unprecedented times.

I want
average,
mundane,
regular,
boring, and
predictable.

I'm reaching for
new,
different, and
better.

Beloved,

You've been hurting for a long, long time. You're trying to find out why you are in so much pain. You're searching for ways to fix what is broken. You're reading books and asking questions. You're talking to friends and even doing research. You're trying so hard to find the truth, so you can fix yourself. In the absence of transparency, vulnerability, and truth-telling by those responsible for your pain, you create conspiracies or stories in your mind. You're trying to:

- **Fill in the gaps**
- **Get clarity and understanding**
- **Heal**
- **Trust the process**
- **Solve our own problems**

You're working so damn hard.

1. Take a few moments and visualize a younger version of yourself.
2. As you arrive in your imagination, notice: how old you are, what you're wearing, where you are in time and space. Take note of who's with you.
3. Stay there.
4. Ask your younger self: what do they need at this moment? What have they always needed?
5. Ask yourself: would it be okay to give myself the love, safety, and validation I've never received?
6. Make a promise to learn how to love and to be present for *You*.
7. Write down every story and belief that's taken root within you, about you.
8. Know that when you create stories about yourself based on your wounds and imagination, you're likely breaking your own heart.
9. Make a promise to work on releasing what isn't true, healing, or aiding in your liberation.
10. Find the truth underneath all the rubble.

I love you. Make a note here of what comes up.

_____

_____

_____

I Know Who I Am

I am
neither slave
nor *Mammie*,
girl
nor ghost.

I am
royalty,
history,
legacy,
a goddess.

I am everything.
I am.
I am.

Does my truth scare you?

Black Power

I am done asking for permission.
I'm allowed to execute,
to expand,
to empower,
and to elevate
my purpose.

**We are allowed to acknowledge our trauma
without allowing it to define our future.**

A Love Letter to Myself

Surely, sweetly, softly,
I think I'll love myself today.
I think I'll make peace with the parts of me
that I keep trying to change.
Today, I'll embrace my body by appreciating
and adoring her.
Truth be told, she's always been so good to me.
Even when I mistreated, punished, and neglected her—
spoke poorly about her—
she still tries so hard to take care of me
and is asking only for me to be good to her
in return.
I think I'll love myself today.
Love the body, love the fat, love the scars,
and remember the history.
My body is the keeper of secrets and of stories
that may never be told.
She is my witness, my living legacy
of wars fought and battles won.
A beautiful reminder that I am *still* here.
I think I'll go love myself today.

When Feelings Do Not Overwhelm

I can feel that
I won't crumble,
and I will not drown.

I won't turn
into flames.

I will not die.
I can feel.
I can *feel*.

I'm living.

Naked is Beautiful

I looked in the mirror and didn't recognize myself.
I asked, "Where did I go?"
I tried to think back to the last time I saw me,
the *real* me...

What happened to the person I used to know?
I drew a timeline, and it pointed me to
my last known location.
To the moments when I became too full of everyone's
opinions, beliefs, and judgements.

I even took on their fears and insecurities, and
wore them as if they belonged to me.

I took on their stories, their memories,
and their blockages, too.
I wore every coat ever given to me.
Until I couldn't recognize myself...

Now I stand naked—full of myself—full of loving *me*—
full of my own wisdom.
Full of my own truth.

Cycle Breaker

It's true.
Sometimes people hurt others
because *they're* hurting.
We can accept this truth and still
show them compassion without
committing to a lifetime of
abusive behaviors and emotional neglect.
I can have compassion and still walk away.

Affirmation:
Life orgasms (overwhelming peace, joy, laughter) will come as a
result of releasing all of the negative weight that I used to carry.

Beloved,

Relationships can be quite difficult.
People will walk in and out of your life,
sometimes with no reason.
It may feel
like your life is a revolving door.

As if there's something wrong with you—
like you're not good enough.
As if you're not designed for "community."

It can make you terrified of being hurt again.

You'll find your people
if you don't give up.
You'll also find yourself
if you don't give up.

Love will come.
Love will grow.
Love will stay.

I love you.

Surrender > Complacency

It's okay
to leave,
to return and then leave again, too.

To discover new lessons about yourself
and to question lies and inconsistencies.

It's okay to speak your mind.
It's also okay to be silent
when all the words
have already been spoken.

It's okay to challenge norms, traditions, *HIS-tory*.

When it's dark,
it's okay to shine a light
on things once hidden.

It's okay.

How would your life be different
if you welcomed the voice of freedom?

To find freedom, you must surrender.

To experience peace, you must surrender.
To gain clarity, you must surrender.

I surrender my will to be right.
I surrender my will to have all the answers.
I surrender my will to have control.

Perfection Doesn't Exist

You will never cross the finish line
if you're chasing perfection.

I don't have to have everything figured out.
I don't have to have all the answers.
I get to say, "I don't know."
I get to be wrong.
I get to make mistakes.
I get to ask questions.
There is so much relief in saying,
"I'm still trying to figure it out."

Use What Hurts

Sometimes,
we learn painful lessons about ourselves
from those who've broken our hearts the most.

We may be tempted
to throw those lessons away
along with the experiences.

Don't.

Use them
as an impetus for your breakthrough,
an ignition for your healing,
and a reminder of the love and respect you deserve.

Want to Know How to Recognize Your People?
Answer these questions:

1. Who knows the *real* you?

    _____

2. With whom do you feel the safest?

    _____

3. Where does your body feel the most present and relaxed?

    _____

4. With whom and where are you free to express
    the full spectrum of your emotions?

    _____

5. Who considers your feelings and needs?

    _____

6. Who is the easiest to talk to?

    _____

7. Who makes you laugh?

    _____

8. Where are you often inspired?

    _____

9. Who would you dance/sing in front of?

_____

10. Who trusts you?

_____

11. Who remembers your history, traumas, birthdays, and anniversaries?

_____

12. Who tells you the truth lovingly?

_____

13. Where are you the most supported and affirmed?

_____

14. Where are you invited?

_____

15. Who keeps your secrets?

_____

16. Who would you call if you received exciting news?

_____

17. Who would you call when you're in a bind?

_____

18. Who would you go on a road trip with?

_____

19. Who would you appear naked in front of?

_____

20. Who would you cook for (as a love offering)?

_____

21. Who would you want to care for you when you're ill? Who would you care for?

_____

22. Who honors your boundaries?

_____

23. Who makes you feel seen?

_____

This is where you place your attention. These are _your_ people.

On Friendship

When I say, "*I love you*,"
what I mean is:

I'm protective of you.
I cherish you.
I thank the Creator for you.
I am *obsessed* with you.
You're not just a *friend*—you are my family, my love.

Daily thoughts of you run through my mind.
I hate anyone who hurts you.
I'm always going to defend you.
I want to date you, spoil you, make memories with you.
Plan trips in my head with you
I want to grow old with you.
I want to hear what you have to say about "this or that."
I look forward to hugging, laughing, cuddling,
and crying with you.

Our conversations are life to me.
I worry about you.
I root for you and support you.
I want the best for you.

I can't get enough of you.
Like water, clean air, and food,
I need you and can't live without you.
Yes, you're that important to me...

If I call you *friend*, know that you are
that and much, much more.

Motherly Advice

If you
are going to do
anything
meaningful,
worthwhile, or
life-changing,

you're going to
have to
just do it.

Just start.
Look fear in the eyes.

You'll have to remind yourself
that you're going to be okay.

You've got this.

The waves
of life are going to come.
But you don't have to be carried away.

This is not the end of your
story, vision, or success.

To all the previous versions
of myself, I love you.

Reader,

What would you like to say to the past versions of yourself?
What do you wish they would have known? What do you love
about them? I invite you to freewrite in the space below.

_____

_____

_____

_____

_____

_____

_____

_____

_____

_____

_____

_____

Pep Talking and Courage Walking

Sometimes, the truth of who you are
reminds people about the truth of who *they* are,
and who they wish they could be.
The growth in you maybe even scares them
Consider their silence, judgment, and rejection
a gift.
Don't worry about it too much.
Keep growing. Keep healing.
Keep learning how to forgive yourself.
Keep confronting fear.
Keep your boundaries. Keep finding your voice.
Keep finding out who you were always meant to be.
Keep living.

In Color

She survived all her traumas
and broken hearts. Promises, too.

She survived the unimaginable, the unpredictable.
The dead wrong *never* should have happened.

She always deserved more and better than she received.
She always gave more to others than they deserved.

She escaped the pain.
She created life on her terms.
Chartered her own path.
Took control of her destiny.
She redefined and reimagined what her life
could be.

Her being here is proof
that she still dreams,
not in black and white or grayscale.
Not with filters of disillusionment or denial, either.
But with equal parts reality, imagination, determination,
and divine feminine power.

The fact that she dreams
in color is proof
that the traumas, the heartbreak, the unpredictable,
and unimaginable
didn't kill her.

She is still *here*...

And she is strong, soft, dreaming,
creating, laughing, loving, and living

in color.

**It's not about who isn't there.
It's about who is here *right now*.**

For RaeD8

You and I
two purple twinkling stars
illuminating an astronomical galaxy,
you in the north
 and I in the south,
a soft collision, destined by fate.
In the cosmos, we dance, we float,
we sing, we sway,
We are reborn—we are free.
Beneath the scars of trauma,
a beautiful tapestry of love, hope, and kindred hearts,
manifestations born of tearful, whispered prayers...
We sing Brandy's "Best Friend."
You radiate my life
in the most meaningful and beautiful way.

Reclaiming Titles

You get to take the word "parents" back.

Who raised you?
Who inspired you?
Who protected you?
Who listened to you?
Who respected you?
Who encouraged you?
Who mentored you?

Those are your parents.
You get to reclaim and rename.

I hope that when you answer these questions,
you don't forget to add yourself.

The title belongs
to those who did the work.
That's who earned the right
to hold the title.

Remembrance

On the hard days,
remember who you love
and who loves you.

Remember their smile, scent, and touch.
The unspoken understanding between you.

Remember who wants you but doesn't *need* you,
who checks on you,
responds to you,
makes you laugh,
and helps you feel human.

Remember who respects you,
listens,
validates the hard shit,
and sees you—the *real* you.

Remember those who
remember you
on the hard days.
Remember.

Only Love

Today, I'm reminding myself
to stay in the arena,

to focus on what's in front of me
and on who's behind me
because the critics never mattered.

Only love does.

Choose Wisely

We are
human—
body,
spirit, and
soul.

We are not a Costco food sample.

No more allowing people
to come into your life
and sample you,
waste your time,
take your gifts
and your magic
for their consumption.

Good Ancestral Wisdom

My brother, Victor, says,
"We are the medicine."
We are.
Remember to be your own medicine.
Be the reason that you heal
from all the things that tried to kill you.

My friend, Judy, says,
"Before colonization, we had love."

Before colonization...
We had each other.
We had *community*.

It's my sincere goal to return to my birthright.

Born to Heal

The day that she was born
is the day that she bore me, too.

She will leave this life
locked in her own *dis-ease*.

I will leave this life
free, healed, and whole.

She was the portal.

I am the truth.

It's Me Time

I am intentional
about my healing
because they're intentional
about harming me.

I am intentional
about my freedom
because they're intentional
about oppressing me.

I am intentional
about loving myself
because they're intentional
about treating me poorly.

I'm intentional
about being a safe person to myself
because they're intentional
about being careless and untrustworthy.

I am intentional
about being unapologetically me
because they're intentional
about wanting me to be like them.

How to be a Safe Space

I love you.
I believe you.
I support you.
I'm thinking of you.
I'd like to help.
I have time for you.
I can hold space for your pain—it isn't too much for me.
I want you to be the most authentic version of yourself.
I respect you.

Monsters Are Real

One of the most important jobs as a parent
is to keep children safe.
To tell the truth
when it's scary,
uncomfortable, and
inconvenient.

One of the first lies that parents tell:
"Monsters aren't real. It's all in your imagination."
[side eye]

What if we all made an agreement
to always tell the truth?
To have hard conversations
and to normalize fear because
monsters *ARE* real, and they *ARE* all around us.

Sometimes, they're in our homes, our closets,
or in the corners of our rooms.
They try real hard to hide in plain sight, but
eventually they make themselves known.

But you don't have to be afraid
when you encounter a monster.

I promise to always protect you,
and I'm gonna teach you everything I know
about protecting yourself.

Our other really important job
is to make sure that we aren't one
of the monsters.

**Acknowledgement *plus* changed behavior
is all the apology I need.**

I Take My Power Back

No human can put a wedge between me and my Creator.
No human can convince me to hate myself.
No human can turn me against myself.
No human has the power or authority over me.
No human knows me better than I know myself.
No human can separate me from myself.

Friends,

Your family will say
you've lost your mind, or that you've
always been a problem.
That you're ungrateful or
rebellious.

Your ex will say
nothing could ever make you happy.
That you're crazy, and
no one will ever want you.
That you're making a mistake.

Your job will say
you don't fit in with the team.
That you're defensive or combative.
No one will ever hire you with that attitude.
You're being problematic.

Your church will say
you're walking away from God.
You're sinful.
You need to repent and change your life.
You're going to hell.

Keep walking in the light of *your* truth.

Permission to Be Okay

In all of your being,
remember to be human.

In all of your doing,
remember to be regular
and enveloped in your okayness.

Remember, it's good and important to:
make mistakes,
fuck it up,
do what you can,
when you can
and nothing more.

Don't forget to be a fucking human.

May You Remember

To all the previous versions of yourself,
may you think of them with tenderness.

May you show up for them in the way
they needed someone to show up.

May you forgive yourself
for what you didn't know,
and for what you couldn't control.

May you remember
that no matter who you were
or what you did,
you were trying to survive.
You were trying to meet your needs
and protect yourself.

You were trying to love yourself.

You deserve
heaps of grace,
tenderness,
and understanding,
too.

Mothering

The day greets me with a soft *good morning.*
She asks,
Will you take care of your body—your first true home?
Will you give me what I need?
Will you take care of me?

Will you...

Wash your face?
Take a shower?
Drink a sip of water?
Rest?
Seek quiet?
Feed your vessel?

Will you take care of yourself before taking care of others?
Will you sit and spend time with yourself?

Today, my answer is *yes—yes—yes!*

You said, "I don't know how to love myself."
She replied, *Then treat me like you treat*
the people you love.

Queer Garden

May I be held, and may I be seen.
Look at me... Don't you dare divert your eyes.
I'm right here.
My showing-the-fuck-up
is a big deal.
Look into my eyes... Feel my energy.
My intention
is to be with you,
welcomed into the fold.

I don't desire to be alone.
I am but a lowly stranger
in need of friends, family, and queer folx
to call my own.
I didn't come to spectate.
I came to commune,
to give as much as I receive
and then some.

I am but a lowly stranger... No, wait!
That's not all that I am...
I'm a sensitive, tender, strong,
loving, beautiful, intellectual, and caring
Black woman
in search of a queer garden,
longing to be rooted in good soil,
pollinated with others who desire the same
friends, family, and queer folx.

I am a Black woman
in need and in search of
truth, wellness, solidarity, and joy.

I am but a Black woman wishing
to be seen, heard, understood, and respected.

Beautiful is what they call me. *Love* is my name.
Beautiful *Love* is
who I am. It's what I am,
and how I care for myself and others.
Otherwise, I'd be an enemy and stranger to myself.

Black Mother-Sister-Friends

Will you be mine?
May I be yours,
Black woman?

I can't tell you how many times
I imagine running to you
into a warm embrace,
arms wrapped
around your body
with your arms wrapped around
mine.

"You're home now..."
The sweet nothings I wish
to hear.

I can't tell you how many times
I imagine
inhaling the scent
of your body.
Your eyes meeting mine
as we burst into laughter.

Sitting next to you,
holding hands as we take
flight to our next destination.
Waking up next to you,
intoxicated by the wonder and beauty
of our sameness.

Black woman, Black sister, Black moms,
Black aunts, Black rebels, Black witches,
Black mothers...
You are my everything.

Black woman,
come to me.
See me.
I love you,
and I want
so desperately
for you to love me, too.

Black woman,
I am hungry
for you to:

Choose me.
Fight for me
Stand with me.
Heal with me.
Spend time with me.

Accept me.
Speak for me.
Surround me.

Laugh.
Dance.
Sing.
Read.
Testify.
Eat.
Pray
with me.

In Defense of Healing

The helpers and healers say, "Feel your feelings."
But some of them don't tell you *how*.

They don't tell you that you have to be willing to sit with
the previous versions of yourself—
the ones who were exiled due to trauma.

You have to sit with it all—
the emotions, thoughts, feelings, and memories.
The ones you've tried to repress
to avoid the enormity of the pain
and because showing emotion or having a reaction
could cause you to be hurt
or punished.

Being in your body was never safe.
Feeling was never safe, either. It was never an option.
You had to stay armored up at all times.
You had to mask as if your life depended on it,
and sometimes it did.

They don't always show you
how to attend to little you, so that you can tell them,
"It's okay to come out now. You don't have to hide.
No one is going to punish or berate you."

We have to tell them,
"No one is coming to hurt you—not now,
and not *ever* again. You can take off the armor,
even if just for a little while."

We have to go back and tell our little selves,
"You are taking your power back.
 You finally get to feel. You finally get
to say whatever you need to say—
your body, your thoughts, your voice...
It's safe now.
I'm going to take good care of you."

Life Is Too Damn Short

Here is what liberation looks like for me...
I live my *hot-messness* out loud.

I remain honest about my failures and shortcomings.
I never give the impression that I know it all
or that I have it all figured out.

I promise, I don't.

Life is too short and too important to pretend
to be something
I'm not.
I try; I fail; I break; I quit.
I feel guilt, shame, and embarrassment
I downplay my accomplishments, gifts, and presence.
I feel intense fear all the time.

I think about freedom and liberation constantly
in the face of capitalism, patriarchy,
trauma, and white supremacy.

This is my truth.

If I'm wrong, I'm *all the way* wrong.
When I'm right, I'm all the way right.
I live my wrongness, my confusion, my anxiety
out loud.

I have a million ways that I protect myself from harm,
from people, and powers that be.
I live on a pendulum of protection and truth.

You'll never catch me performing or doing a little dance
for the powers that be.
I show up as *me*... Take me or leave me
right where I am.
My practice of showing up as real allows other people
to show up authentically and vulnerably.
I learned a long time ago that this builds trust
and helps me to find my people.
The people in my life feel connected,
free, and at home—
this is what I hear often.
When they are with me, they're safe.
They can be themselves without excuse
or apology.
How I show up is my offering to mutual and collective
liberation.
This is how I express my love and build
community.

I am so glad that I chose to heal out loud,
so that I could love out loud.

There is nothing better than freedom.

Love Is

Everything I learned about love,
I learned it by loving myself.
I learned by accepting love from those precious souls
who know how to love.

Find someone who loves you and then go live your life.
Often, we run from love, and run away
from the chance to be loved
because we're so afraid of it not being a for-sure thing.
So afraid of the what-ifs.
So afraid of the proverbial shoe dropping.
So afraid of *everything*.

We look for the 100%,
reject the 80%.
But the truth is,
the 80% can feed your soul
to such a degree that it makes
you FEEL like you've found the 100%.
Like you're whole
and safe.
Like your life adds value, meaning, and purpose.
As if you could do and be anything—
allowing you to live to fight and live
to thrive another day.

Perfection is stupid, and it's not real.
It was created to keep you chasing.
To keep you feeling deficient.
To make you believe you will never
be good enough
or have enough.

In love and in life there is no perfection.
There is only truth.
Trust in your own enoughness.

Perfectionism cancels authenticity
every single time.

Pep Talk

Pick up the phone.
Your gift is calling.

What belongs to you
is only for you.
Pick up the call.
Your gift is trying to reach you.
Use it, share it, and release it.

Follow inspiration.
Follow curiosity.
Follow your truth.
Follow your passion.

It's not *too late*.
You aren't *too old*.

You're still breathing.
You're still dreaming
Keep going.

Too much time has *NOT* passed.
Take one small step.

There is room.
There is need.
There is desire.
Your gift is waiting on you.

Pace yourself.
Breathe... Rest... Sleep...
Eat... Journal...
Make a list.
Make some time
to make your dreams count.

People need what
you want to offer.

Keep your eyes on *you*.
Don't look to the right
or to the left
to see what others are doing.
Mind your business and
mind your craft.

Others may be doing
something similar,
but they can't
do it like you do.

This is your time—the
universe is conspiring
to make you a beautiful success.

Saving yourself simply means being committed to working toward a way of life that is for **your** greater good.

I Am

At some point in life,
I stopped explaining why
I am who I am.

I was born into this.
Traumatized by this.
Healed into this.

I evolved into this.
I was forced into this.
I mothered myself into this.
I loved and nurtured myself
into who I am.

Though I labor alone, I am not alone.

Reader, although you may feel alone in this season of life or in what you are experiencing—I invite you to write freely about why you are actually *not* alone and who and what is supporting you.

_____

_____

_____

_____

_____

_____

_____

_____

_____

_____

_____

_____

_____

The pain.
The pleasure.
The discomfort.
The unknown.
The changes.
The healing.
They all go together.
It all matters, ushering us into our becoming.

Lasting Love

I wish someone would have told me
I can be anything I want in this life,
including free.

I can be anybody
including myself.

I can *and* will make the best decisions for myself,
ones that change the trajectory of my life and my world.

It will hurt like hell
and feel good—like home—all at the same time.

The people whom I love the most
or want to love me the most
may not ever understand me
or know the real me.

They'll likely will only accept the *me*
that they knew before, so they'll
resent me for doing what's best for me.
Criticize and
reject me, and
even turn on me as if the love between us
never existed.

But at some point,
love,
freedom,
family,
true safety,
joy, and
happiness will come—
like an answered prayer.

They will all come and stay.

Winning

At this point in my life,
I'm walking in my privilege and
in my entitlement.
I don't want to do anything
that I don't want to do.
I survived all my traumas.
I didn't just survive, either.

I won.

I write about my wound.
I feel my wound.
I respect my wound.

I take care of myself
and my community.
I was born into oppression,
but I found my freedom.

I'm not going to do anything
that I don't want to do.
I've earned the right
to live freely.

Psilocybin Lessons

The world is in a crisis.
The whole damn world needs healing.

Some people are starting wars.
Some are starting fires.
Some are starting the next generation of trauma.

Some of us are starting a revolution.
We are *not* the same.

Finding Purpose

You'll find your voice in the unfamiliar,
in the moments when your stomach churns,
overwhelmed with fear and *dis-ease*.

You'll find your purpose and your destiny, too.
Don't give up or say *goodbye* to what you need or desire.
You deserve the life and liberty calling out to you.
Keep an open mind and an even more expansive,
curious heart.

You'll find your answered prayers
of love, peace, and abundant offerings
in the unknown and unrecognizable.

You'll find connection.
You'll find flow.
You'll find yourself
in the new and never been done before.

Be ever so grateful for the traumas and the traditions
that weren't transferred to you.
When you begin to question
the once unquestionable
and as the once certain becomes uncertain,
let it be.

Turn toward your fear
instead of away from
the unfamiliar that is calling you...

This is BIG

It's no small thing to survive.
It's no small thing
to keep going,
living, or to develop
the language and the courage
to name your pain
for yourself or others, or
to take up for yourself.

It's no small thing
to confront your abuser, or
to make friends with your anger.

It's no small thing to leave
and start again,
to create a new community or family.

It's no small thing to move from merely
existing to living and then
eventually, thriving.

This is all to say that I'm proud of you. I love you.

To Everyone I Love

I'm never going to stop saying these three words:
"I love you."

On a spectrum of how well I know you—
from complete stranger to closest living relative,
partner, or best friend,
it doesn't matter.
I feel it in my body. I feel it in every part
of my heart, and to the deepest recesses
of my soul.

"I love you."

I'm never going to withhold love.
Don't ask or expect me to
because I've never regretted showing love.
Love has never treated me poorly
or given me a reason to fear it.

Loving people has never come back to bite me.
Loving people has never caused me pain.
Loving people will *never* be my downfall.

It's all the other shit that makes love difficult.
The moments when I'm wounded
by another person's unloving actions.
When I'm in a grief or depression cycle.
When my trauma tries to protect me.
The moments when I ignore my intuition,
or take more than I can handle.

The moments when I don't speak up for myself.
The times I'm unaware of how and when I hurt others.
The moments when my ego is running the show,
or when fear and other emotions stand in opposition to
and in replacement of love.

Love is solid.
It's safe.
Love lives within me.
I love you.
I do.

Letting Go of Fear

Let us relax
into love.
Come here.
Lie next to me.

Don't you want to be loving, too?
Don't you want to stop choking back the words
that you really want to say?

Don't you want to be
soft?
Affectionate?
Present?
Held?

Come with me—let's be loving together.

Midlife Reflections

The older I get, the more I want to hold
onto everything beautiful.
The more healed I become, the more
I sense the beauty in others around me.

Trending Topics

The term *soft life* became popular in 2023. Millions
of women resonated with the dream, and the
innate desire to live a softer existence.

What does that mean for me?

It means living a life that is all about the blanket life—the
cuddling life, the restful, slow-day life, the comfort-food
life, the financially-abundant and flowing life, the multiple-
orgasm life, the queering-out-loud life, the travel and vacation
life, the indulgent, hedonistic life, the open-expression-
of-love life, the working from a place of joy instead of
working from a place of need, freedom life—free to take
space, free to speak and be heard, free to exist in my curvy,
voluptuous body life. The free-to-be-my-Black-self life.

Leaving a Healed Legacy

Some people spend their whole lives wounding people.

They spend their whole lives doing the hurting...

Others spend their whole lives helping people.

They spend their whole lives healing people...

It's always been clear to me that I want to live
and die being a healer, spreading seeds
of hope, curiosity, love.

May those of us who are helpers
heal this wounded world together.

The Afterlife

I won't do anything
that I don't want to do.
I'm too busy
finding *Me*
and too focused
on what I want
and need.

I'm too busy spending time
with those who make me feel
good, *real* good.

I'm too busy
focusing on *Me*.

I don't have time for anything that doesn't matter.
Not for words and conversations
that are too cool or too *surfacy*.

I'm busy feeling.
I'm busy writing.
I've got a lot
to say,
to learn, and
to do.

I got a lot of livin' to do before it's too late.
Won't you come with me?
Let's get busy living, loving, and healing together.

All the Wrong Advice

Have you ever been told,

"Don't say, '*I love you*,' unless you mean it"?

Well, I love you, *and* I mean it.

When I say *I love you*, what I mean is...

You're really dope, and I'm pleased to know you.

I'm also really glad you were born.

I enjoy our time together.

You inspire me to be *and* do better.

Our relationship matters.

I think of you often.

I want to support you in any way that I can.

I value our open and honest communication.

I feel safe being vulnerable with you.

Proximity will never change the way I feel about you.

My Therapist Parts

You were a burden to them.
You're not a burden to me.

You were an inconvenience to them.
But you're not to me.

Your truth was too *truthful* for them.
But I can handle your truth, and I believe you.
Your emotions were too much for them.
But I am 100% comfortable with your emotions.

You were invisible to them.
But I see you, and I love you.

Life After Heartbreak

I spent a lot of my life in a sea of pain.
Focusing my attention on the people who hurt me.
Creating stories about why they hurt me.
Fantasizing about what would have been different
if the hurting had never occurred.

I spent a lot of time demanding answers from God:
"Why Me?"

The focus on the pain kept me isolated,
stuck, and confused.

This next phase of my life centers on what is right
in front of me.
Who loves me?
Who supports me?
Who belongs to me?
Who do I belong to?
Who *and* where is my community?

Phoenix

The bedrock of finding out who you are
often derives from knowing who you are *NOT*.

I am *not* them.
I am *not* like them.
That is *not* who I will become.
This trauma, these memories
are *not* the end of my story.

Affirmation

Repeat after me:

My body belongs to *me*.

My time belongs to *me*.

My voice belongs to *me*.

My choices belong to *me*.

My sexuality belongs to *me*.

No one has power over *me*.

No one controls *me*.

I am whole and complete.

Be still and know—your life is not over.
Be still and know—your story is still being authored.
Be still and know—life can get better.
Be still and know—your life has value.
Be still and know—we need you.

Loving myself is an affront to white supremacy culture that tries to teach me to hate myself.

I love myself.
I love myself.
I love myself.
I love myself.
I love myself.

Creator's Rebellion

You keep expecting me
to write about you,
think about you,
and be inspired by you.
Even to tell the world
about you.

But I keep writing
my history,
my truth,
my pain,
and my experiences.

Who else can write for me?
Who's gonna tell *my* story?
Who's gonna sing *my* song?

You?

'Cause somebody has to speak for me.
I can't write for you.
I'm too busy focusing on *me*.

I'm going to love myself so completely that I'll never
doubt my place in the world again.

Who's gonna protect me?
Me.

Who's gonna provide for me?
Me.

Who's gonna love me?
Me.

Who's gonna speak up for me?
Me.

Real Self-Care

Real self-care is revolutionary, rebellious, and resistant.

Real self-care is a lifetime of recovery from
the violence of white supremacy.

Real self-care is a ritual, a way of being, not a coping skill.

Steps to Loving and Caring in an embodied way:

- I will recognize the impact of trauma, capitalism,
  and colonization on how I exist in the world.
- I will challenge heteronormative and
  cisnormative beliefs within me.
- I will change my binary thinking.
- I will spend time in nature
- I will seek help from the energy of well
  ancestors (known and unknown).
- I will prioritize the Self within me.
- I will honor my emotional, mental, physical,
  spiritual, and financial capacity.
- I will listen to my mind, body, and intuition.
- I will name when enough is enough.
- I will flow into my community for care.
- I will honor the need to keep some
  parts of me to and for myself.
- I will prioritize pleasure, play, and fun.
- I will rest often and as needed.

Power

I'm a superhero
with superhuman powers.
Immortal like Jean Grey,
telepathic like Professor Xavier,
regenerative like Wolverine,
independent like Captain Marvel,
with the stamina, strength, and beauty of Shuri.

I'm a superhero
with superhuman powers.
At least, that's what I tell myself.

I'm a time traveler
landing at the right place
at the right time
to fix the first ancestral wound.
The first incident of
abuse,
poverty,
dis-ease,
addiction,
parental alienation,
incest,
sexual assault,
violence.

When I heal,
you heal, too.
I'm a superhero.
You're a superhero.
Let's change this world.

A Love So Hot

She says, "Don't speak.
Just feel."
Staring into each other's eyes, she says,
"Lose control."
My body's tight.
She says, "Baby, relax."

Reminding my mind to focus,
I'm willing my body to obey.
Repeatedly, I whisper,
"I'm safe. She's safe."

Our hands? Moving.
Our tongues? Slow dancing.
Hips thrusting
back and forth and
side to side.

She says, "May I..."

Lick?
Suck?
Touch?

You know where...

She's asking for direction and permission to:

Rub.
Stroke.
Squeeze.
Hold me here.

Safety over seduction is the way to my heart.
The intimacy, passion, love,
and respect—it's a goddamn **inferno**.

The Sweetest Love

Love sees me.
Elevates me.
Listens to me.
Checks on me.
Understands me.
Shines a light on me.
Lifts me.

Fear hides me.
Silences me and mutes me.
Shrinks me.
Builds walls around me.
Cancels me.
Distances me.

Give me love.
Give me love.
Give me sweet
love.

When you feel yourself rising in love with me,

pause and know that

the feeling is mutual.

The Best Yes

Before you,
I couldn't comprehend the enormity
of being in love.
I couldn't believe in it for myself.

After you,
I found myself lost in dreams
of our forever story.

Because of you,
I'm happily invested in love.
I'm busy being loved.
I am ignited by love.

If love is an ocean,
we're falling to the depths
of our healing.
If love is an ocean,
we have only one choice,
and that is to
surrender.

If love is an ocean,
we're submerged, rising, swimming, and floating
together
in Black, beautiful, bold, soft, sapphic love.
Your love
is a *heartgasm*
to my soul.

It is a love
that
climaxes,
tingles,
burns,
spasms,
electrifies,
creates tension,
throbs,
vibrates,
paralyzes,
releases, and
relaxes.

Keep coming...

My Gryffindor

I've never wanted the days to be longer until I met you.
Can anyone come and stop the time?
May we love until our last breath,
reincarnate
and finish what we started,
taking nothing for granted,
treating each day as a gift,
loving each other and spreading love all around.
I would live this life again if it meant I could
spend each day loving you.

Building Differently

You're teaching me
about love,
about all that fake shit
that doesn't matter.

You're teaching me
to focus
and listen,
to be intentional
yet considerate,
to relax,
release,
to stay present
and connected.

With you, I want to stay present.
Hear every word.
Remember every experience.

I want to build.
Plan.
Dream.

I can dream.
It feels safer now.
Life is sweeter with you.

You're teaching me how to live out
the best years of my life.
You've given me a reason to believe in love.

Fairytales Are Very Real

In my fairytale happily ever after...

You make me believe in a deeper love—
a serious and intentional love.

You make me wonder, and dream,
and see a glimpse, even a glimmer
 of the future.

You make me *soooooft*, mushy, and giddy,
like a teenager.
You are my crush, one of my closest friends,
my lover, and my
partner.

You've given me all the reasons
to believe in love after heartbreak.

My Forever

If I'm eating a persimmon for the first time,
I want to share it with you.

If I'm taking time off work,
I want to spend it with you.

If I can trust and share my secrets with anyone,
it's always you.

You are my first thought when I awaken in the morning.
You are the last thought before I drift off to sleep.

You are in between everything.
It's always you.
I love you.

Ready for Love

She calls me
her *person*.
Even told her friends and family about me, too.
She says she wants to protect me
and give me the world.

She's secure in herself.
She's secure in who I am.
She supports my dreams.
No matter how much time we spend together,
it's never enough.

I always want more, and more, and more.
I wish time would stand still.
I love her.
I love me.
I love...
this little life.

Intimacy

Come with me.
Let's be naked.

See inside of me.
Penetrate me
like only true love can.

My body is your ocean.
Dive into me,
carrying nothing
but truth and pure intentions.

Go deep with me,
leaving anything unreal on the surface.

Partnership

Find someone who listens
and who remembers...

The things that you want to forget.
The things that are important.
The things that make your life easier.
The things that make you happy.

Love doesn't have to be complicated.
It gets complicated when ego and unhealed trauma
both ruin
the best made plans,
the best relationships, and
the best futures.

Healthy, Happy, Healing Love

She came into my life
softly, gently, and intentionally.
A force made of nothing but love,
and it feels like I am breathing
for the first time in my life.

My Gift

If love is medicine,
you are my prescription.

If this is my one chance at a life partnership,
you are my forever person.

It breaks my heart when I consider
the possibility of you being absent from my life.

I am seriously in love with loving and building a life
with you.

For life.

I

2024

It's funny how Goddess revealed you were the one.
Wearing those red pants—passport in hand.
It was always you.

What if it works out? It will.
What if we live the rest of our lives in love? We will.
What if we never have to heal
from another broken heart? We won't.
What if we live the rest of our lives
laughing, loving, and living our dreams? We will.
What if we are each other's best decision? We are.
What if we change
each other's lives—for the better? We already have.
What if we create heaven right on earth? We are.
What if every road was always leading us
into each other's arms? They were.
What if we have finally found a life
worth living? We have.

I have family.

I have deep, enduring friendships.

I have a life partner.

I am living my dream.

Reader, I am whole.

I am the best thing that's ever happened to *me*.

I asked Goddess, "Would you make something beautiful from the remnants of my trauma?"

She said, "I did—I made you. You've made something beautiful out of the mess, and that is fucking beautiful."

Beautiful Human,

When I started writing this book, I didn't know whether it would be a book of meditations, affirmations, prayers, or poetry. Nor did I have a clear vision of what I wanted this to become. I only knew I needed to keep writing my wounds, thoughts, and lessons for *us*.

I envisioned you reading each page, highlighting and *amen-ing*, as I often do when reading something that resonates deeply. I knew how to begin but couldn't figure out how to end—except to end it with love.

I wrote from my personal experiences as this is the only way to transmute my healing into something useful. As with my memoir, *What Children Remember*, I have given you my grief, shame, and secrets. I hope you use what I have gifted you to free yourself *and* someone else.

As I write this on January 2, 2024, I am smiling and grateful. Some days, a part of me (my ego) believes I know more than you and everyone else. On other days though, I'm led by an opposing part of me that is wholly convinced that I know nothing.

The truth exists in *both* parts of me, and I am a forever learner and truth-teller.

What I learn, I promise to teach. What I receive, I vow to give it away. This world is not my final destination, so I don't plan to take anything with me. If this book has helped, guided, or encouraged you, please send an email to: tashahunterauthor@gmail.com or tag me in a post on Instagram or Threads **@tashahunterlcsw**.

If you feel so inspired, leave a review on Amazon, Goodreads, or Instagram. This will help my work to reach the beautiful souls who need it most.

I love you forever,
tasha hunter

Gratitude

Thank you to my ancestors and Goddess for working in concert to instill in me the courage I would need to speak, write, teach, and lead.

To my therapist, D.G., for being the safest person I've ever known and for walking with me as I step into the woman that I am today.

To my small and supportive Instagram community, thank you for every comment, like, and share that moved me to publish this book. You showed me that my people are out there and need what I have to offer. You affirmed and motivated me to keep tending to my wounds.

Readers, thank you for reading this book that chronicled my healing. Thank you for sharing my book with your communities and supporting my work.

My editor, Mellisa Felix—you said yes. Thank you for walking beside me, patiently speaking new life into the parts of me that needed to know: I *am* a writer. You consistently called me "writer." What a mother, sister, and friend you have been to me through this process.

Simon Walker, thank you for creating my book cover. Your patience, kindness, and gentle spirit meant the world to me.

Andrea Miller, you are my closest friend. Thank you for being my chosen family. I love you.

My friends, I could not have made it this far personally or professionally without you. You have witnessed my pain and my healing. I stand straighter because of you.

To Chris, Kya, Irie, and Imani—my first real family, my first real home. Words cannot adequately express how you have given my life purpose. You have anchored me, and I love you.

To Rox, you came into my life right on time. You are my favorite person. Our love is a dream come true. It's you and me, now and forever. I love you, baby.

About the Author

@tashahunterlcsw

tasha hunter (she/her/we) is a Black, queer listener, healer, writer, teacher, and advocate. She is a liberation-centered mental health therapist who specializes in working with Black women, femmes, and LGBTQIA communities.

tasha is a Level 3 Certified Internal Family Systems therapist who approaches healing from a non-pathologizing, decolonized lens. She most often provides a safe container for individuals seeking help due to generational trauma, ancestral trauma, inner child wounding, sexual violence, racism, sexism, oppression, sexual identity/romantic relationship stressors, and spiritual/religious deconstruction. tasha's clinical practice also includes pre- and post-integration of psychedelic/ entheogenic medicine experiences, breathwork, somatic practices, spirituality, and ancestral wisdom.

tasha is the author of the memoir, *What Children Remember*. Her writing has been featured in *She Lives Her Truth* and *please cut up my poems*. She is the host of the podcast, *When We Speak*. She lives in North Carolina and owns a mental health private practice.

Made in the USA
Las Vegas, NV
02 September 2024

94676238R00175